The Magic Kingdom

Property, Monarchy, and the
Maximum Republic

The Magic Kingdom

Property, Monarchy, and the Maximum Republic

Dan Hind

Winchester, UK
Washington, USA

First published by Zero Books, 2014
Zero Books is an imprint of John Hunt Publishing Ltd., Laurel House, Station Approach,
Alresford, Hants, SO24 9JH, UK
office1@jhpbooks.net
www.johnhuntpublishing.com
www.zero-books.net

For distributor details and how to order please visit the 'Ordering' section on our website.

Text copyright: Dan Hind 2014

ISBN: 978 1 78279 403 5

A CIP catalogue record for this book is available from the British Library.

Design: Stuart Davies

Printed in the USA by Edwards Brothers Malloy

We operate a distinctive and ethical publishing philosophy in all
areas of our business, from our global network of authors to
production and worldwide distribution.

CONTENTS

For my brother, Matthew

A Constitutional Crisis

The cleverest politician cannot subjugate those who only wish to be free.

Jean-Jacques Rousseau

When Britain's finance-dominated economic model collapsed in 2007 and the state bailed out the banks, what in normal times passes unremarked became undeniable. The state is the single most important factor in determining the distribution of material goods within the territory it controls. Through the operations of the central bank and the institutions of law enforcement, the state stood revealed as the ultimate arbiter of outcomes in the economy. The state enabled grand larceny in the financial sector and then coordinated the getaway.

Mainstream coverage has shied away from what the collapse taught us. Rather than denying what is plainly true those who dominate public speech have taken refuge in nonsense. The BBC tells us that quantitative easing is like putting 'imaginary petrol' in our cars.[1] Politicians resort to the occult principle 'as above, so below', and talk about 'the nation's credit card' or they exploit the Sadean possibilities of concepts like austerity.[2] When particularly lurid crimes come to light they are dubbed scandals.[3] It is a symptom of the crisis in which we find ourselves that public speech regularly descends into desperate euphemism and appeals to magical thinking.

But despite all the extravagantly misleading analogies, the secret is out. The state allocates rewards and applies penalties. It inflicts pain and confers pleasure, exults some character types and forms of conduct, degrades others. It seeks to determine who knows what, and who can speak with some expectation of being heard. Around it congregate legitimating stories that are also tickets to sustenance for the tellers. The state seethes with mutually reinforcing fictions and fantasies. These stories form part of the state. They are how business is conducted, how the show goes on.

The state is avid for facts about the population and energetically infiltrates a nominally independent civil society. It finds, and lavishly rewards, partners in a nominally private economy. As I write, civilized men and women in official agencies are doing their best to ensure that nothing threatens what they understand to be national security. Yet their account of what constitutes national security is as secret as their work to defend it.

The bailout of the financial sector and the subsequent revelations of widespread criminality in the political and economic directorate mark the beginning of a constitutional, as well as an economic, crisis. After all, bankocracy is a form of the state and replacing it will entail deep constitutional change. This is not widely acknowledged in the easily available circuits of communication. Instead we have been subjected to an energetic exercise in distraction, in which themes that appeal to an unreformed public opinion are being mobilized to prevent the obvious from becoming politically relevant.

Our current arrangements can no longer be defended by anything resembling a reasonable argument. And those who dominate speech no longer try. Instead they use a mixture of cheap tricks and esoteric learning to keep the population befuddled and divided. The Coalition government has pitted public sector workers against private sector workers and mobilized resentment against welfare recipients and immigrants. The Labour opposition has refrained from questioning the fundamentals of the government's programme and has been content to wait until the 2015 election, when it will promise hope and change without troubling voters with too many details. It can scarcely afford to be too explicit, given its own responsibility for the financial sector's wholesale collapse, and its continuing commitment to a political settlement that converts public passivity into extravagant financial sector profits.

Though this shared crisis management has so far been successful, there are grounds for thinking that it is the kind of success that begets failure. The state is openly acting to preserve the power and wealth of the financial sector. The financial interest has become, in the official mind, the national interest. For politicians to talk about market forces and administrative expertise now seems ridiculous. Their efforts to impersonate the ruled are falling flat.

In a system that prides itself on its representativeness this is a problem. People are on the brink of wondering if the state that underpins and protects a few favoured interests might be remade as an instrument for securing the common good. They will remain on the brink for years yet. This is the heart of the constitutional crisis: we no longer recognise the impersonation of the national mood offered by Parliament via the BBC.

How this crisis is resolved will determine the future of the country. The odds will always favour what R.H. Tawney called 'the oldest and toughest plutocracy in the world'. But the outcome is only foregone if we decide that it is. The current arrangements are indefensible and we all know it. Perhaps there is nothing we can do to change them. But not to try, not to draw on every resource we have, seems too disgusting to contemplate.

Introduction

The Needs of Oligarchy

We have been taught not to like things. Finally somebody said it was
OK to like things. This was a great relief.
David Byrne

This book argues that republican doctrines and habits of mind
provide valuable resources for those who want Britain to become
more democratic, more equal, and more truly prosperous. They
also provide a means of uniting the fragmented majority that
wishes an end to bankocracy and the regime of crime. It sets out
to convince by first subjecting the existing constitution to a
process of destructive description, and by then drawing the
outlines of a modern republican constitution. Anything useful
will be soiled with much use. Republicanism is no exception and,
if *The Magic Kingdom* is to persuade, it must scrape away some of
the junk.

The argument does not concern itself much with the
monarchy. But the standard meanings of the words 'republic' and
'republicanism' in British English oblige me to say something
about the Crown. It is never easy to forget that Britain has a
crowned head of state. In 2012 the Diamond Jubilee and the
London Olympics made it impossible. We saw our Queen on a
barge on the Thames and apparently leaping from a helicopter
into the jamboree for the New Jerusalem that was the games'
opening ceremony. The Prime Minister David Cameron made the
connection explicit in his New Year message in 2012:

The coming months will bring the global drama of the Olympics and
the glory of the Diamond Jubilee. Cameras and TV channels around
the planet will be recording these magnificent events. It gives us an

extraordinary incentive to look outward, look onwards and to look
our best: to feel pride in who we are and what – even in these trying
times – we can achieve.[1]

Cameron is on easier terms with the Palace than any of his recent predecessors. He sees in the institution a device with which to reconcile the country to the austerity – 'these trying times' – he claims is necessary. More profoundly, he wants to use the monarchy to bind people to an economic and political settlement in which the power of the financial interest is confirmed and the reorganization of British society begun by Margaret Thatcher is made permanent.

The Coalition government, backed by much of the rest of the British apparatus, the Loyal Opposition, the press and the BBC, used first the Jubilee and then the Olympic games to promote the idea of Britain as the shared endeavour of diverse peoples. For a precious few weeks in the summer of 2012 the roars from the stadium drowned out discussion of a shaky government's controversial programme. It was a lesson well learnt. In the years ahead the emotional resources of monarchy will be deployed in defence of a political order that can survive only so long as that discussion is deferred.

Most British people are happy enough to have a crowned head of state. According to a *Guardian*/ICM poll in May 2012 69% of the public think the country 'would be worse off without the monarchy, while 22% say the country would be better off'.[2] Support for abolition has been steady at around 20% for the last two decades according to Ipsos Mori. In the Jubilee year this fell to 13%.[3] Given these figures, efforts to recapture the Olympic spirit of wordless unity will doubtless continue to give the Queen a high billing. In 2014 the Crown can be expected to take a prominent role in commemorations of the outbreak of the First World War.[4]

Those who want to abolish the monarchy and replace the

Queen with an elected President go by the name of republicans. They can occasionally be heard in the responsible media, as voices of complaint at moments of national celebration. In the highly choreographed exchanges that characterise public life in Britain, the appearance of monarchy calls for its proper, dissenting response. Someone will be found to insist that the country will never be right until it more like somewhere else, France, say, or the United States. The conventions observed, both sides go about their business. The great majority of sensible people enjoy themselves, taking pleasure in the way the world is, while an eccentric few have another kind of fun, gnawing away at their sour abstractions. This is how we like our controversies, predictable and reassuring. *Cosy*. My intention here is to describe another, less familiar and more substantial, republicanism.

It might seem strange to deny that republicanism and anti-monarchism are the same thing. But there is something much stranger about a political culture that can only bring itself to discuss republicanism in the context of its vestigial monarchy. The extent to which we conflate anti-monarchism and republicanism in Britain, or more precisely in England, is highly unusual, even unique. It is as though the continued existence of the monarchy in its current form gives us permission not to think seriously about the systems of government that have replaced it almost everywhere else in the world.

Instead of discussing the substance of public sovereignty – what it means for a people to be self-governing, what it means for a people to be effectually free – we content ourselves with a debate about the personal qualities of the Queen, the antics of some of the more spirited members of her family and the relative merits of continuity and modernity. Republicanism is reduced to a manageable scale, to become a particularly eccentric faction of liberal opinion. Here too, public speech takes on an air of nursery nonsense. Anti-monarchists calling themselves republicans propose changes to the constitution that are not in formal terms republican and that would confirm the power of a small number of politicians, civil servants and private actors.

Some critics of the monarchy worry about the culture of deference that the institution promotes. A hereditary head of state makes a mockery of the idea that we are the authors of our own destiny and legitimates a much wider pattern of inherited privilege. The institution stifles ambition and poisons social relations. But if we want equality of opportunity, then the evidence suggests that equality of condition is the most pressing consideration. Denmark manages to have a monarchy and high levels of social mobility. But it is also much more equal than Britain. America is a fitfully democratic republic and is even more unequal than Britain. Most people aren't persuaded that abolition is the royal road to social justice and they are right to be sceptical.

Others argue that, by appearing to stand above party competition, the monarchy legitimates the content of that competition, that it keeps controversy in proper bounds. Its claim to be apolitical puts electoral politics in its place and protects a very particular, and highly political, idea of the nation. If you oppose monarchy you can be denounced for hating your country. Meanwhile, gigantic powers – the military and the intelligence agencies, the Bank of England, the institutions of law and order, offshore finance in the City and the Crown Dependencies – huddle in the shadow cast by a diminished crown.

There is more to this idea. But the monarchy serves an even more consequential purpose. It draws attention away from the core of the existing constitution and acts as flypaper for the radical imagination. The person and personality of the monarch obscure and protect the Crown-in-Parliament, the organizing principle and sovereign power of an unreformed and deeply exotic state. The monarchy enrages and befuddles the opponents of the existing order and pushes them to oppose the great majority of their fellow citizens. Advocates of democracy

7

blunder into a vote they cannot win. Principled opposition to the current shambles is tempted into irrelevance by the continued existence of the Crown.

Every oligarchy faces the same problem. It must prevent those it excludes from uniting and demanding inclusion. So it tries to ensure that the majority fails to understand it. Further, it seeks to obscure the form of government that haunts and terrifies it, republicanism at full stretch, what we might call the maximum republic. But while the problem is the same everywhere, each oligarchy must find its particular, usually national, solution. The British version of oligarchy has an important asset in the Crown.

In America the nation and the flag, the military and the Christian faith are all pressed into service, in order to prevent a formally sovereign people from discovering and exerting themselves in their own interest. Empire frustrates republic through a constant exertion, a costly and elaborate regimentation of sentiments both liberal and conservative, blue and red.[5]

In Britain, too, oligarchy survives through astute appeals to both conservative and liberal impulses. Red and blue again, even if the colour scheme is reversed. But the monarchy supplies part, an important part, of the necessary obfuscation, by acting as a focus, a point of obsession, for the reforming imagination. The English republican is permitted public speech only to rail against Ruritanian incidentals. The great, apparently casual, popularity of the Queen prevents discussion of the origins and structure of power. The Queen is both the most conspicuous element of the unreformed constitution and worst place to begin the work of reform.

Republicanism in the strong sense I will describe is about much more than anti-monarchism. Indeed, it isn't about anti-monarchism at all. This will strike some readers as eccentric or even offensive. But it ought not to be so impossibly difficult to imagine that a fully sovereign people might want to keep a crowned head of state. I am willing to leave the decision to a body politic that understands its options and is free to decide for itself. If such a body politic wants the Crown to remain while insisting on its own supreme power, this should hold no terrors for a republican. Whether the Crown would accept such an arrangement is another matter entirely.[6]

Republicanism seeks to remake the state as the shared possession and achievement of a sovereign public. Once we consider republicanism in these terms, we do not have to choose between a popular monarch and a republic.[7] Radical change to the constitution of the state, and hence to the distribution of knowledge and power, need not abandon the inherited forms. It does not have to set itself against the affections of the majority. On the other hand, a republicanism that inveighs against cakes and ale holds few terrors for our masters.

Our options are not exhausted by sentimentality about the person of the monarch and its mirror image, outrage at this same sentimentality. We can very easily find a place for a crowned head of state in a thoroughly republican constitution. But those hostile to monarchy too often lend the little weight they have to the momentous confusion they say they oppose. It is time to do without the satisfactions of an essentially phony confrontation, so we can grasp the conflict that matters, between democracy and oligarchy.

At the moment the opponents of oligarchy in Britain are divided and preoccupied at best, at worst actively hostile to one another. Republicanism can provide the majority with a shared critique of the existing order and a coordinating agenda. But it will only do so if it is understood in terms that reach beyond the flesh of appearances into the guts of how our lives are currently administered by others.

The natural, unforced meaning of the word republican in Britain tells us something about the country's unacknowledged legislation, the poetry through which the existing order convinces itself and others. A few know that republicanism is not the same as anti-monarchism. For the most part they are tucked up tight inside the tangle that this book aims to unpick. If those of us on the outside can grasp the distinction then we begin to articulate a new constitution.

The current organization of the state, consisting as it does of a mass of statutes, habits, immemorial principles and hasty improvisations, provides a playground for a certain species of conniving intelligence. What is uncodified can be slyly deformed in what is sometimes, revealingly, called the national conversation. The first two chapters of *The Magic Kingdom* set out to describe the governing settlement and the political economy over which it presides, the better to appreciate both their strangeness and their coherence.

We're not supposed to pay much attention to these things. They are meant to go without saying. But we need to talk plainly about our system of government, even if doing so can seem simple-minded or impolite. The obscurity of our arrangements provides cover for rampant criminality and abuse. Public life takes the form of a series of carefully organized robberies and assaults, in which the political order is thoroughly implicated. In such circumstances the act of description transforms what it describes, by drawing attention to the tacit understandings and whispered asides that form part of its fabric. Meanwhile reticence and irony serve as pillars of the unreformed state.

The Magic Kingdom sets out the form and merits of republican government and suggests how republican principles might be embodied in a new constitution, a new relationship between the state and the people. This is not a matter of making Britain more like somewhere else, like France or the United States. Nor is it a matter of tidying up some of the messier anachronisms. It is about establishing a maximally republican form of government, in which each citizen has both power and the knowledge needed to exercise it.

Republicanism consists in common ownership of the state.

But the scale and composition of the political nation has changed since republican principles were discussed in classical Rome, renaissance Florence and revolutionary America. Thanks to advances in scientific and technological understanding, nations have become immeasurably more wealthy and productive. States have become larger and more complex, their power far greater. The conditions of common ownership can only be satisfied if we take into account this new power and complexity.

Popular ownership of the modern state will not be secured if we limit ourselves to the established categories of classical constitutionalism. There is more to a constitution than the legislature, the executive and the judiciary. The systems of communication, subsidy and credit are achievements of state power, as are the artificial persons that dominate material production and exchange. At the moment when such things are mentioned at all they are usually treated as matters for technocratic administration, as facts of nature, or as the unchallengeable outcome of competition in free markets. In this way much of our political discussion becomes a kind of efficient gibberish, wrong but useful. Republicanism itself must be thoroughly renovated if the idea of the state as a common possession is to be more than a pious-sounding fraud. If we do not encompass the whole of the constitution of the state in our discussion we are only tinkering.[8]

There's more to this work of revision. Republicanism has its origins in a world of radical inequality and violent prejudice. There is much that is repulsive in it. The patriarchal and elitist assumptions that riddle the republican tradition need to be picked out if its fundamental principles, and the energy they generate, are to be made generally available. A republicanism worth having is a feminist, anti-racist and egalitarian republicanism.

If we reject republicanism outright because of its history we give up useful resources. Worse, we leave those resources in the exclusive possession of those who think us unworthy of public status and will do all they can to keep us confused and disunited. Better to take reasoned and unsentimental possession of a tradition that, for all its many faults, has magnificence in it.

Not only that, republicanism has found expression in English, in ways that make it useful here and now. We are unlikely to persuade our fellow citizens if we set ourselves against what they know and love about where they live. Our current rulers work hard to exploit the affections of those they rule and set them against any change in conditions. With a little care we can align the desire to belong with the inclination to be free.[9]

The final chapter sets out how a republican agenda in Britain might be advanced over the next few years. The referendum in Scotland and the General Election in 2015 both offer opportunities to those who no longer wish to make their lives in a crime scene. But it is in a properly republican programme that the best chance of successful reform resides. An independent Scotland that reproduces the Westminster model in one country is less attractive than a Scotland in which each citizen has an equal share in the state, and where public debate includes, and indeed centres on, the vital interests of the people as a whole.

By breaking the silence that surrounds the constitution the Scots threaten more than the Union with England. They are disturbing the complexes of sentiment and consent on which the unreformed state in Westminster rests. In the aftermath of the referendum on Scottish independence there is a chance that constitutional reform will re-emerge as a political cause in the rest of the United Kingdom. The Scots will not secure English, Welsh or Northern Irish liberty. But the movement for Scottish independence poses a threat to oligarchy in all of the United Kingdom. After all, if the Scots can escape Westminster-Whitehall, the City of London, and the BBC, then why can't everyone else?

As things stand the general election will take place less than a year after the referendum. We now have the means to communicate among ourselves and find common ground in ways we have only just begun to appreciate. The old methods of control have withered and the new ones are not yet securely in place. Competition in the Parliamentary system is not sufficient as a response to problems that cannot be addressed adequately by the powers of a Parliamentary majority. But a republican movement that resists the blackmail implicit in our electoral system and engages with it nevertheless will threaten the existing parties with extinction. This threat of extinction in turn will make possible the deep reform we need. Parliament is not a prize to be won, it is a puzzle to be solved, one constituency at a time.

Edmund Burke wrote that 'it is more easy to change an administration than to reform a people'.[10] But while reform might be difficult it is necessary. We are what the unreformed constitution has made us, with its schools and newspapers, with its tunes and turns of phrase. If we want to change the constitution, we must first change ourselves. This means setting aside the temptation to identify with national politicians chosen by the dominant parties and made familiar through the operations of the print and broadcast media. It means taking advantage of the opportunities to communicate and coordinate with others online while remaining wary of the techniques of surveillance and manipulation now being piloted. The republican tradition offers us a way out from the nauseating complicity and insinuating appeals to sentiment that characterise so much of our public life. It is, as we shall see, a tradition characterised by suspicion as well as candour. We will need both in the years ahead.

This, then, is a republican text that is not anti-monarchist. The mere fact that we have a crowned head of state does not seriously impede the creation of a substantive republic, or a socialist commonwealth for that matter. To imagine that it does opens up a vast field for the exercise of a style. It is fun to cry 'death to kings' and spit defiance at hereditary privilege. Readers looking for such a thing can find it in Christopher Hitchens' *The Monarchy: A Critique of Britain's Favourite Fetish.* First published in 1990 it is as fresh and urgent now as it was then. Which tells you most of what you need to know about romantic anti-monarchism.[11] There is more fun to be had in the patient discovery of our current arrangements, even more in the steady work of replacing them.

While the politics of Britain suggest that it is time to revise these arrangements, the economics loudly insist on it. For more than a decade the state-owned Bank of England allowed the financial sector to increase the supply of credit and run up unsustainable debts. Once confidence collapsed the same state-owned institution reduced real interest rates below zero and spent £375 billion buying bonds from the country's bloated and anaemic banks. What was blandly called a programme of quantitative easing saved those who caused the problem in the first place. Since then the Coalition government has shifted the costs incurred onto the rest of the population.

We are accustomed to hearing that constitutional reform is not a 'bread and butter' issue. But the powers of a country's central bank are a matter of deep constitutional significance. The £375 billion created by the Bank of England could buy enough loaves to reach from here to Mars and back, with change for butter. 12 Quantitative easing is only the latest variation on the theme of financial sector dominance. This dominance was established, and has been maintained, through the actions of state institutions. These institutions have caused some to win and ensured that others lost. All this passes unremarked in constitutional debate because constitutional debate has become a site of mystification and misdirection. The main parties will not draw our attention to the relevant facts. We do not help matters if we keep our attention fixed on the House of Windsor, that light from a long dead star.

The Magic Kingdom is a response to local conditions. It is an attempt to challenge a particular oligarchical arrangement. But what happens in Britain is not a merely local matter. Just as Prussia was once described as an army with its own country, modern Britain is best understood as a complex of globalised finance companies with its own country. The business coalition represented by the City of London is dedicated to the cause of free trade in a regime of private property. In Geoffrey Ingham's words, the City seeks to remove 'the substantive obstacles to absolutely free exchange which the existence of independent nation states presents'.[13] The central task of the existing British state is the promotion of the financial sector's interests at home and overseas. It seeks to make London and its offshore satellites attractive to foreign capital and to make the global economy safe for the businesses that convene in the Corporation of the City of London.

London's banks and trading houses defend the interests of the wealthy around the world against the claims of democracy. The place is, in important respects, the capital of global capitalism. As we have seen in recent years this means it is also the capital of organized crime. The apparent solidity and timelessness of the unreformed settlement are central to London's status. As the Citibank executive Walter Wriston once observed, the trade in dollars outside the US 'exists in London because people believe that the British government is not about to close it down. That's the basic reason and it took you a thousand years of history'.[14]

A republican movement for constitutional reform will draw attention to the hidden wiring that connects London to global capital flows and their enabling circuits of information and untruth. To the extent that our current economic arrangements frustrate popular sovereignty in Britain, they must be changed. And so renovated republicanism here threatens the cause of financial oligarchy around the world. Social democrats and socialists in Europe and North America, in Latin America, Africa and Asia have a stake in what we do. Perhaps, if challenged effectively, footloose global capital will leave. This is to be welcomed. Perhaps part of the financial sector will join them. This too is to be welcomed. Let those who want to make their living from crime, or from providing services to criminals, do so elsewhere.

Subordinating the economy to the rule of law is only part of the challenge we face. Material production needs far fewer of us than they once did. Our current rulers respond by turning the shared world into a casino. Images of personal liberation overlay the lived experience of debt and low pay for the majority and spectacular wealth for a ruthless or lucky few. The production of celebrity incarnates the lie that we too could have had a life worth living, if only we had tried a little harder, had believed in ourselves a little more fervently. By contrast, public status gives us the means to exchange what Richard Sennett has called 'the spectre of uselessness' for work in which we secure both personal emancipation and the common good.[15] Such work is only possible if we reconstitute the state on republican lines.

This is not a matter for a few representatives, fitfully applauded or catcalled by a distracted public. Politics in a fully realised republic becomes the stuff of steady application, careful revision and dedicated endeavour by large numbers of us. We are paid for the work we do and are rewarded for our contributions. Our application does not depend on an outbreak of unnatural selflessness. It derives from self-interest properly understood. The universal achievement of citizenship provides the great majority with our best hope of material improvement.[16] And this achievement of citizenship begins when we set aside trust in our representatives and trust ourselves instead.

There is enough ambition in the British for us to want to matter, enough virtue to justify the ambition. But we do need to rid ourselves of some comforting fantasies. We cannot idle our days away in contemplation of a revolution that will not happen, or work furiously for reforms that will make no difference. We cannot afford to ignore the electoral system, any more than we can afford to become engrossed by it.

Perhaps above all, we must do without the comforts of an internationalism that is a mutation of the ideology of the late empire. To act on a national stage, to seek change in the country where you live, is not to turn your back on the world. It is, rather, to reject the fantasy of high moral purpose and transcendent values that provides the current empire of crime with its most plausible-sounding alibis.

There is great work to be done here. A new democratic politics in a stronghold of financial oligarchy would be glorious in itself and would give material and practical assistance to people elsewhere. Imagine, a republic built on the wreckage of 'the oldest and toughest plutocracy in the world', secured by the efforts of a people long kept dejected and deceived.

Chapter I

A Time-Honoured Improvisation

British rulers think the country has a native problem ... The truth is
that the natives have a ruler problem.
Anthony Barnett

Let's start with a question. Is Great Britain bigger, smaller, or the same size as, Britain? An ornithologist will tell you that a Great Snipe is bigger than a plain old Snipe, so the tidy-minded might want to say that Great Britain is bigger than Britain. On the other hand, those better acquainted with the country's pragmatic approach to life might conclude that 'Britain' is no more than an abbreviation of 'Great Britain' – they are the same place, and hence the same size. But the rationalist and the pragmatist would both be wrong. 'Britain' is synonymous with the United Kingdom of Great Britain and Northern Ireland, but 'Great Britain' refers to the largest island in the British Isles and, perhaps, some of the smaller islands surrounding it. Ireland, north or south, is not part of Great Britain. But Northern Ireland is part of Britain. So it follows that Great Britain is smaller than Britain.[1]

As we move from the generalities of human geography to the specifics, the uncertainties only multiply. Scarcely one British person in a hundred could give a clear and accurate description of our country's system of government. If pressed they might float the idea that they live in a constitutional monarchy that is also a democracy. But as a matter of flat-footed fact, the United Kingdom of Great Britain and Northern Ireland is neither. No clear principle fixes the monarch in a constitutional order. Rather, the reigning king or queen is still formally sovereign. Parliament legislates, and the Cabinet governs, in his or her name. Monarchical power has, for most practical purposes, been appropriated by those able to command a majority in the House of Commons. But this so-called Crown-in-Parliament falls far short of constitutional monarchy.

Sovereignty means that nothing – not tradition, not law – can put the Crown-in-Parliament in its place and keep it there. It follows that the country isn't a democracy, either. The people are not sovereign because the Crown-in-Parliament is sovereign. The democratic elements in the system are established by legislation that any Parliamentary majority can repeal.

Nigel Lawson, a former Chancellor of the Exchequer, describes what British democracy means in practice. 'Essentially', he writes, 'it is the means by which the people are provided, at regular intervals, with the opportunity peacefully and constitutionally to remove a government in which they have lost confidence'. In this system oppositions become governments when people lose confidence in the incumbents. It echoes Joseph Schumpeter's famous definition of democracy as an 'institutional arrangement for arriving at political decisions in which individuals acquire the power to decide by means of a competitive struggle for the people's vote'.

In such a system governments do what they think best and are judged on the results as reported in the media. It is a conception of democracy that lends a useful liveliness to elite competition but does not seriously challenge the supremacy of the Crown-in-Parliament. Indeed some have gone so far as to proclaim, as Enoch Powell once did, that 'we are not a democracy, we are a parliamentary nation'.

This is to speak of things as they are, without their usual bodyguard of conventional understandings and customary terms of reference. But to approach the political settlement unaccompanied by the normal evasions is to enter a wilderness. Much that appears solid turns out to be flimsy, much that is almost invisible carries the weight of the whole. Attempts to discuss matters frankly soon run into a thicket of informal prohibitions that have the force of a taboo.

Plain speech, being a breach of social convention, can be ignored rather than debated, since the foundation of our arrangements is precisely what *goes without saying*. From the point of view of the insider, plain speech is necessarily inaccurate, since it misses the roles that irony and discretion play in the governing settlement. To say out loud what is best passed over in silence is to demonstrate an unforgiveable gaucheness. Instead of a response the literal-minded can expect only a wince. Propriety requires an absence of candour.

But let's remain in the world of fact for a moment, nevertheless. Alexis de Tocqueville said that 'in England the constitution can change constantly, or rather it does not exist at all'.[2] The remark reveals a great expanse of open ground between Britain and the rest of the world. For if, like Tom Paine, we think that a constitution 'has not an ideal, but a real existence; and wherever it cannot be produced in visible form, there is none', then Tocqueville is right and Britain doesn't have a constitution.

In *The Rights of Man*, Paine provides a definition of what it means to have a constitution that has become fixed as a 'standard signification' almost everywhere in the world, apart from Britain:

A constitution is a thing antecedent to a government, and a government is only the creature of a constitution. The constitution of a country is not the act of its government, but of the people constituting its government. It is the body of elements, to which you can refer, and quote article by article; and which contains the principles on which the government shall be established, the manner in which it shall be organised, the powers it shall have, the mode of elections, the duration of Parliaments, or by what other name such bodies may be called; the powers which the executive part of the government shall have; and in fine, everything that relates to the complete organisation of a civil government, and the principles on which it shall act, and by which it shall be bound. A constitution, therefore, is to a government what the laws made afterwards by that government are to a court of judicature. The court of judicature does not make the laws, neither can it alter them; it only acts in conformity to the laws made: and the government is in like manner governed by the constitution.[3]

There is nothing that relates to the British government as the laws relate to the judiciary, since there is nothing that stands above the Crown-in-Parliament, least of all the judiciary. In the words of Tom Bingham, a former senior Law Lord, 'Parliament has no legislative superior. The courts have no inherent powers to invalidate or strike down, supersede or disregard the provisions of an unambiguous statute duly enacted by the Queen in Parliament, and indeed, an extremely limited power to inquire whether a statute has been duly enacted'.[4]

So much for the facts of the matter. Let's now look at how the British government describes itself. In 2011 the Coalition under David Cameron published *The Cabinet Manual*, which set out for the first time 'the conventions determining how the Government operates'. The document is in no doubt that we have constitution. The Prime Minister himself tells us that 'this country has a rich constitution developed through history and practice'. And something called 'the UK constitution' even has it own heading, tucked in after the section on 'Parliamentary democracy'. The order of precedence seems right, somehow.

Although the Prime Minister's introduction talks of the *Manual* 'codifying … the conventions determining how the Government operates', the main text of *Manual* insists that 'the UK does not have a codified constitution'. On the other hand, its authors do seem to think that there is more to the constitution than convention only. In fact, according to *The Cabinet Manual* our 'rich constitution' consists of laws made in Parliament ('statutes'), the 'Royal Prerogative', 'judicial decisions', 'conventions', and 'European and international law'.[5]

As noted above, judicial decisions may form part of the

gorgeously embroidered fabric of British public life but they have no power over laws made in Parliament. European and international law are said by the *Manual* to 'inform and influence the UK's constitution'. This sounds reassuring but, again, it reflects nothing but the authors' good intentions. Bingham is in no doubt that the sovereign power of the Crown in Parliament allows it to break treaties and international law as it sees fit. As for conventions, which the *Manual* describes as 'rules of constitutional practice regarded as binding in operation but not in law', the document in no way explains how they can be 'binding in operation but not in law'. Whether they are in fact ever binding is a matter to which we will return shortly. Needless to say the document makes no attempt to codify them, despite the Prime Minister's confident claims in the introduction.

The Cabinet Manual sees no difficulty in claiming that the UK is both a 'Parliamentary democracy' and a 'constitutional monarchy'. In this it is squarely in line with other official accounts. A government White Paper from November 2001 *The House of Lords – Completing the Reform*, provides more detail on what the government means by these terms. In the section 'The Pre-Eminence of the House of Commons', we learn that 'sovereignty rests with the Crown in Parliament. Law making rests with the sovereignty of the Crown in both Houses of Parliament'. In practice, it goes on, 'the powers of the three parts are uneven' since the House of Commons is the 'pre-eminent constitutional authority within the UK'. Elected on a universal franchise, this pre-eminent House of Commons 'enables the people to give a clear and unequivocal answer to the question, "Whom do you choose to govern you?" The UK's political system is built around that principle.'[6]

And yet, as so often in Britain, things are not quite as fixed and stable as they seem. Enabling the people to give a 'clear and unequivocal answer' to the question of who governs no longer seems quite the foundational principle it once did, now that we have a Coalition of Conservatives and Liberal Democrats. We certainly don't come across anything like this in *The Cabinet Manual*, where we are told instead that 'elections are held at least every five years to ensure broad and continued accountability to the people.'

Instead of unequivocal clarity we must, for the time being, make do with broad accountability. Given that, to quote from the *Manual*, the UK constitution 'has evolved over time and continues to do so', this shouldn't surprise us too much. We build our political system around principles that come and go. Doubtless we will see a renewed emphasis on clear and unequivocal answers when a single party once again commands a stable majority in the House of Commons.

It is a longstanding convention that strong Prime Ministers can cast aside longstanding conventions when it suits them. When the Conservatives took power in 1979 they arrived with a comprehensive plan to reorganize the country's political economy. This plan prompted resistance from Labour councils who sought to offset the effects of spending cuts through increases in the rates levied on property. Although in opposition the Conservatives had worried about the dangers inherent in a highly centralised form of government, this did not stop them from drawing more power away from the periphery in ways that would have been straightforwardly unconstitutional in a normal country. Ferdinand Mount, a contrite veteran of those early days of Thatcherism describes how casually local government was stripped of its financial independence:

> ... *when I was working for Margaret Thatcher , I was sent off to the Department of the Environment to devise a means of capping the domestic rates. The Deputy Secretary, Terry Heiser, warned that, if we went down that road, local government would never be the same again. 'But Terry', I said, 'it's only going to be temporary'. Of*

course it wasn't, and thirty years later, local government is still a pale and neutered shadow of its former self.[7]

A simple vote in Parliament was all that was necessary to make a change that would have required a constitutional amendment elsewhere. Similarly, when the new forms of municipal socialism being developed by the Greater London Council proved electorally popular, the centre abolished the capital's coordinating authority.

The Conservatives under Thatcher considered the old civil service an obstacle to reform and consciously sought to 'de-privilege' it. A structure intended to guarantee impartiality was altered to bring market-mimicking pressures and incentives to bear under the rubric of New Public Management. Whether one agrees with the changes or not, there is no doubt that they radically altered conventions that should have been 'binding in operation if not in law'.

A connoisseur of the British way with paradox might think that the Conservatives monopolise impatience with long-established conventions. But Labour can be every bit as insouciant. Andrew Rawnsley describes how Tony Blair handled the transfer of responsibility for setting interest rates from the Treasury to the Bank of England in 1997:

Handing over control of monetary policy was, by any standards a sensational step, and the more so because it had not been advertised in advance either to the electorate or anyone else in the Cabinet. When the Prime Minister allowed him into the secret, Sir Robin Butler was astounded to learn that Blair and Brown were planning to act without consulting other ministers. The Cabinet would not meet until two days after the announcement. Butler suggested to Blair that his senior colleagues should be involved in such a momentous change. The Prime Minister wasn't interested in giving the Cabinet a vote. 'I'm sure they'll all agree,' repeated Blair, more emphatically. Butler made a final attempt to convince Blair to follow what Britain's most senior civil servant regarded as the constitutional proprieties. 'How do you know that the Cabinet will agree with the decision when it's still a secret?' Blair replied very simply: 'They will'.[8]

Not surprisingly, when asked by a politics student what the British constitution was, Butler answered that 'it is something we make up as we go along.' It would perhaps have been more accurate to say that the Woosters in the Prime Minister's inner circle crash about doing whatever the can get away with, while the Jeeveses in the civil service do their best to tidy up after them.

The pace of change under Blair led some commentators to declare that we now live under a new constitution. Devolution in Scotland and Wales, the incorporation of Human Rights Act, and the use of referenda, once set in the context of the European Communities Act of 1972, are taken as forming the beginnings of a body of fundamental law.[9] Critics of New Labour have also complained that Blair's presidential style of government marked a significant break with the old constitution. But the system has always been remarkable for its protean quality. Remember the first half of Tocqueville's remark, 'in England the constitution can change constantly'. Blair and his successors have not dared to tamper with the fundamental principle of the British way of doing things, the sovereignty of the Crown in Parliament. Referenda have become conventional, with all the certainty and security that the word implies. It might be difficult to alter the laws governing the relationship between Britain's constituent parts or to repeal the Human Rights Act or the European Communities Act. But they are no more immune to the force of a vote in Parliament than any other legislation.[10]

Given the extreme flexibility, not to say bonelessness, of the current settlement, the whole business of government is attended by considerable uncertainty. One academic study notes that, in discussions concerning the relative power of the Prime Minister and the Cabinet, 'the memoirs of leading political figures, as well as commentators, are frequently contradictory'. As we can see above, Blair, like many Prime Ministers, blithely assumed he could do pretty much what he liked and bring the Cabinet onside after the fact.

While politicians in government are happy to dispense with some conventions, they take others extremely seriously. They insist that it would be wholly unconstitutional to allow the members of their own parties to instruct or direct them. The Labour Party's members have been notably unsuccessful in turning formal control over the party's programme into influence over what Labour governments actually do. And politicians are even more convinced that immemorial principle exonerates them from any particular attentiveness to public opinion between elections. There is certainly no mechanism, other than Parliament and the blunt instrument of the election, to hold governments to their promises and manifesto commitments.

The peculiarities of the British system also play a part in keeping politicians insulated from popular pressures. The sovereignty of the Crown in Parliament confers an intimidating mystique on the Commons and on those who have mastered both its procedures and the apparatus of publicity that surrounds it. The Labour MP David Kirkwood described the awe he felt as a new arrival in Parliament in 1922:

I had to shake myself occasionally as I found myself moving about and talking with men whose names were household words. More strange it was to find them all so simple and unaffected and friendly. In the House of Commons there is no snobbery, except among the third-raters.

No wonder Winston Churchill pronounced Kirkwood 'a grand fellow, if handled the right way'.

We can reconcile observable reality – Britain doesn't have a constitution – and the official version – Britain has an uncodified constitution – easily enough if we stop using the 'standard signification' for the word constitution offered by Paine and accepted in the rest of the world. One way of doing this is to concede that Britain doesn't have a 'modern constitution', but that it is endowed instead with a 'traditional constitution'. This is the approach taken by Martin Loughlin, the Professor of Public Law at the London School of Economics, in *The British Constitution: A Very Short Introduction*. There he explains that:

> *The essential point is that the traditional and modern concepts have different objects: the modern constitution has as its object the office of government, while the traditional concept has that of the state. The modern concept distinguishes between governments and society, whereas the traditional concept suggests that the manners, culture, and traditions of a people form the 'real' constitution of the state.*[11]

Loughlin draws heavily on Edmund Burke to explain what he means by a 'traditional constitution', particularly the 1770 essay, *On the Present Discontents*. Burke argues that:

> *Nations are not primarily ruled by laws; less by violence. Whatever original energy may be supposed either in force or regulation, the operation of both is, in truth, merely instrumental. Nations are governed by the same methods, and on the same principles, by which an individual without authority is often able to govern those who are his equals or superiors, by a knowledge of their temper, and by a judicious management of it ... The temper of the people among whom he presides ought therefore to be the first study of a statesman.*[12]

Here Burke echoes the great Scottish philosopher David Hume, who argues in *Of the First Principles of Government* that 'as force is always on the side of the governed, the governors have nothing to support them but opinion'. Hume points out that even when the population as a whole is unarmed, the ruler must rely on something other than force to make his soldiers obey: 'the soldan of Egypt or the emperor of Rome might drive his harmless subjects like brute beasts, against their sentiments and inclination: But he must at least have led his mamalukes, or praetorian bands like men, by their opinion'.[13]

To understand the temper of people is to know how it is to be governed. And while Burke acknowledges the importance of laws in maintaining sound government, he attached far more weight to the personal qualities of the governors than to formal rules of government:

> *Constitute government how you please, infinitely the greater part of it must depend upon the exercise of the powers which are left at large to the prudence and uprightness of Ministers of State. Even all the use and potency of the laws depends upon them. Without them, your Commonwealth is no better than a scheme upon paper; and not a living, acting, effective constitution.*[14]

The British state, according to Burke, is of a piece with its people. Effective government depends on the ability of statesmen to manage the tempers of the governed and their virtuous ability to act on 'public principles and national grounds'. Statesmen must study the nation's history, and learn the language of custom and unbroken tradition with which to craft their appeals to a nationally shared 'common sense'.

If Burke is to be believed, statesmanship is a matter of dangling hooks baited with arresting phrases in front of that great fish, the public. Once the fish is caught, those who induced it to bite can concentrate on bringing their personal qualities to bear on the formal mechanisms of the state. Judicious management of the temper of the people combines with the conscious experience of prudence, uprightness, and superior understanding. It is a delicious cocktail for those who aspire to a high place in the world.

Even a very short introduction to the British constitution must make a move like Loughlin's if it is to stretch further than a few sentences. And, to be fair, there are rules in British politics, some of which are quite constitution-like. It isn't entirely unreasonable to talk of a British constitution. But it is important nevertheless to register the deep strangeness of the British system, when compared with the rest of the world. We live in one of the very few states on earth that manages without a legible constitution. Unlike the rest of Europe, British society has, in the words of Larry Siedentop, 'continued to seek unity in manners rather than ideas. It has discouraged discussions of ideology, preferring to rely on civility as the cement of society. "Decency" and "common sense" have been its watchwords.'[15]

It is as though we have divided the world in two. In one half is Britain, with its traditional and unexceptional arrangements and in the other is everyone else, with their newfangled deviations from the (British) norm. What's odder is that we still like to think of ourselves as the model and archetype of good government. We tell ourselves that ours is mother of Parliaments and that Britain is the cradle of liberty and representative government, even though almost all the countries in the world organise their affairs on a radically different basis. The conceit forms part of the language of statesmanship. As such it can expect to pass unchallenged in the circuits of communication constructed around, and for, Parliament. We live on an island, but even so, this might be taking things a little too far.

Loughlin's explanation has the merit of capturing something of how the British system operates day by day. Politicians never tire of talking about the feelings and concerns of the electorate. Left and right draw on different emotional resources to marshal their own troops. But the real battle, the grinding war of electoral attrition, takes place over the so-called middle ground. Politicians describe one thing after another as an outrage to *ordinary, hard-working families,* or something that *all fair-minded people* will support. The *decent majority of men and women up and down the land* are constantly invoked in opposition to out-groups of scroungers, immigrants and layabouts whose size and significance are left deliberately vague. Our leaders much prefer the lush meadows of sentiment to the tundra of fact.[16]

But this talk of a traditional constitution is still a little confusing, for the rationalist and the empiricist alike. There's no plan, of the type favoured by Americans and continental Europeans. But, for all the talk of the traditional constitution as what Loughlin calls 'an inheritance, a partnership between, past, present and future', the record describes a history of breakneck improvisation. Prime Ministers have trampled conventions they found inconvenient. Whenever possible they have done so by administrative fiat. When necessary they have resorted to the sovereignty of the Crown in Parliament.

The confusion that surrounds the country's political arrangements has long been part of how this traditional constitution works. In his *Reflections on the Revolution in France* Edmund Burke worried that 'sophisters, economists and calculators' were destroying 'the glory of Europe', its 'mixed system of opinion and sentiment' with 'its origin in the age of chivalry':

> *All the pleasing illusions which made power gentle and obedience liberal, which harmonized the different shades of life, and which by a bland assimilation, incorporated into politics the sentiments which beautify and soften private society, are to be dissolved by this new conquering empire of light and reason.*[17]

Burke predicted that the founders of the new regime in France would soon have to rely on violence to protect the institutions that they had 'disembodied' in the name of reason: 'in the groves of their academy, at the end of every vista, you see nothing but the gallows'. His prescience is often noted. But notice, too, the role he assigns to 'pleasing illusions' in the business of government. Tall tales about a timeless constitution are part of the sales patter of a properly briefed statesman. And there is something else. Burke believed that the sentiments of private society should be incorporated into politics by means of these illusions. Power, by being personalised, is made if not likeable then tolerable.

A century later Walter Bagehot durably reworked the Burkean idea of the constitution as a mixture of workaday reality and romantic fiction. *The English Constitution* of 1867 divided the state into dignified and efficient elements. In Bagehot's telling the House of Commons was 'the true sovereign' that appointed the 'real executive', that is the governing Cabinet.[18] Meanwhile, the Queen, or better yet the Royal Family, put on a show of grandeur and continuity. More than that, the royals reflected and sanctified the lives of their subjects. This is what Bagehot meant when he wrote that 'a princely marriage is the brilliant edition of a universal fact'.[19] The British monarchy, to repeat Burke's phrase, 'incorporated into politics the sentiments which beautify and soften private society'. It is not enough that a people defer. To be made durable, deference must be made personal. It must seem like the good-natured accommodations of a loving family, rather than the means by which some take and others give in an unrelenting series of depredations.

The Crown served a valuable, and acutely political, purpose in the late nineteenth century. The monarchical pageant didn't only lend romance to the national life. The bulk of the population – those Bagehot dubbed 'the vacant many' – actually thought that the Queen ruled. The responsible and more highly evolved classes – 'the inquiring few' – knew differently. The country he described was one where 'the appendages of monarchy have been converted into the essence of a republic' but where 'it is needful to keep the ancient show while we interpolate the new reality'.[20] This is why Bagehot famously warned that 'we must not let in daylight upon magic'.[21]

Bagehot writes that 'the working classes contribute almost nothing to our corporate public opinion, and therefore, the fact of their want of influence does not impair the coincidence of Parliament with public opinion'.[22] He scarcely mentions women and the title he chose, *The English Constitution*, gives us some idea of how much he thought of the other nations in the United Kingdom. If the country was a republic it was one whose body politic was educated, propertied, English and male. Since then the masses he thought unfit for elective government have won the vote. To accommodate this change the sedative comment that surrounds the constitution has also changed. After all, even the modern equivalents of 'the peasants of Dorsetshire', Bagehot's 'miserable creatures', know that the Queen isn't the country's ruler.[23] And so we are told that we live in a democracy that is also a constitutional monarchy. Universal suffrage requires more magic, not less. The crown still acts as auxiliary but the pleasing illusion that is truly indispensable is the fantasy that the people rule.

In order for the official version to be true, we would have to have a constitution. And this constitution would have to be consistent in its own terms and demonstrably effective in establishing the rules that govern the public life of the nation. But what we have at the moment would no more persuade a loveable English empiricist than a supercilious French rationalist. The British do not have a constitution in theory or in practice. We have a warehouse full of conventions and customary understandings. And up and down the dark aisles stalks the Crown-in-Parliament, dressing itself as it pleases, discarding what it dislikes. And far, far away in the darkness are places where the Crown-in-Parliament, awesome though it is, fears to tread.

Of course, much of our legislation does have a constitutional appearance, insofar as it relates to matters that other countries set out in their constitutions. We have laws that establish who can vote in elections, how central government relates to local government, and so on. So it does look as though at least some of the rules concerning government are written down. Hence some are inclined to say, as *The Cabinet Manual* does, that Britain has an uncodified constitution. In other words, we have all the elements of a constitution, but we've never bothered to set them out in an orderly fashion. But when people talk of an uncodified constitution they might just as well say that the constitution is encoded. Most of us are unfamiliar with the code, and our unfamiliarity is integral to it. Our ignorance is a resource to be husbanded and preserved as far as possible. For all its longevity, the political settlement cannot long survive bright sunlight.

According to Burke and his many followers, Britain does have a constitution, albeit one made not of words on paper but of a mysterious ectoplasm called 'the temper of the people'. The hooting and wailing we hear are the voices of our ancestors, bringing the wisdom of the ages. According to Paine and his party, all this talk of a traditional or uncodified constitution is a sheet thrown over the matter in question. We don't have constitution and the sheet floats and takes on a spectral life through an elaborate system of wires and pulleys.

For a people that makes much of its sturdily empirical turn of mind and love of history, it is surprising that this sharp difference of opinion between Tom Paine and Edmund Burke excites so little interest. It is all the more remarkable when we consider that Paine has won the argument in most of the rest of the world while being largely forgotten in the country of his birth, and that Burke's party appears to have won here not by an appeal to evidence, but by locking up their opponents or driving them into exile. For simplicity's sake, let's say that we do not have a constitution, and turn to a closer examination of the country's political economy.

Chapter 2

CSI: UK

The City regards itself as separate from the country at large, and sees the actions of the government as somehow not binding on it.
Anthony Hilton

This, then, is the place where we live. The fundamentals haven't changed since Bagehot wrote, though the relationship between the dignified and the efficient has shifted slightly. The monarchy is no longer as important as a source of authority. It still naturalises the present arrangements and gives a time-honoured aura to a form of government characterised by bewildering mutability. But democracy has replaced Queen Victoria in the imaginary constitution of those whose ignorance of the structure of the state forms part of the foundation of that structure. The notion that we already live in a democracy leaves reformers complaining about gothic or neo-gothic holdovers that most people find endearing or reassuring.

Of course, the move to universal suffrage has had important consequences for the conduct of politics. While the House of Commons still chooses the executive, it does not pretend to do so by assembling some dominant fraction of an active public opinion. Instead, elections lend dignity to a process whereby one group of party managers struggle with others to secure the excitements of executive office in an unexamined political economy. Rather than discussion of fundamentals, electoral competition consists of appeals to sentiment and material self-interest, 'eye-catching initiatives'[1] and hysterical demonstrations of party unity.

In the years since the financial crisis broke, the mainstream parties have remained resolutely committed to competition in these terms. Politicians nobody trusts leak stories that nobody reads about rivals with whom they have no significant ideological differences. It is a model of politics that works in the absence of serious problems. Politicians alternate warnings about imaginary threats with talk of the rewards they will give the electorate if they give them power.[2]

As the franchise expanded in the late nineteenth and early twentieth century the zone of the political miraculously contracted. Once bondholders had to share the vote with the rest of the population, money in particular became a subject hemmed in with taboo. Elected politicians earned a reputation for seriousness when they declared finance outside the realm of politics. As far back as 1929 Philip Snowden, the Chancellor of the Exchequer in the first Labour administration, told his party that 'in the control of credit and currency, the administration of the control must be kept free from political influences ... Parliament is not a competent body to deal with the administration of such highly delicate and intricate matters'.[3]

Even after the 1945 election, when Labour decided that Parliament was competent to deal with such highly delicate and intricate matters and nationalised the Bank of England, they did not think to explain the significance of what they were doing to the electorate. Throughout the postwar period, the management of the economy remained in the hands of technocratic administrators whose authority rested on a generational mandate that expired as those who had fought in the war retired or died.[4]

The slump in the thirties and the experience of national coordination in the Second World War changed the balance of power in Britain. But this change was not inscribed in the structure of the state. Writing in the 1960s, the Cabinet Minister Richard Crossman remarked that while 'social democracy consists of giving people a chance to decide for themselves':

This philosophy is extremely unpopular, I find, with most members of the Cabinet. They believe in getting power, making decisions and getting people to agree with decisions after they've been made. They have the routine politician's attitude to public opinion that the politician must take the decisions and then get the public to acquiesce. The notion of creating the extra burden of a live and artic- ulate public opinion able to criticise actively and make its own choices is something which most socialist politicians keenly resent.[5]

The great political mobilisation of the mid-century put Keynesian technocrats in control of the commanding heights by changing the composition of Parliament. It did not bring economic – let alone monetary – policy under any kind of general supervision. Regulation was tight and effective, so much so that the chairman of Lloyds, Lord Franks, complained to the journalist and author Anthony Sampson that 'it was like driving a very powerful car at twenty miles an hour'.[6] But the state retained its orientation towards finance and the Wilson government's attempt to break the Treasury-BoE-City grip on economic policy failed. Over time the banks steadily and stealthily regained their unaccountable powers, with consequences that are all too visible.[7]

Nowadays only a handful of elected politicians take any interest in economic matters. Lobbyists and officials vastly outnumber these few and have little difficulty persuading them that what they tell them is all they need to know. Bryan Gould, a member of the Labour Shadow Cabinet in the late eighties and early nineties, has written that:

I found that most of my colleagues had no knowledge of economics and either steered well clear of economic policy – preferring to concentrate on more general topics such as foreign or social policy – or else they swallowed whole the current orthodoxy since they had no capacity to take an independent view.[8]

Today most MPs don't know how the British economy works and

would be baffled if someone suggested that they ought to find out. The financial sector constitutes the governing interest in matters of economic policy and it exerts its influence in partnership with the most intellectually impressive elements of the permanent administration, the Bank of England and the Treasury. This domination by the financial sector of economic policy is reflected in, and reinforced by, media coverage, where bankers vastly outnumber any other group as authoritative sources in both the print and broadcast media. One City source interviewed by an academic researcher confided before the crisis broke that 'the national financial press are written for the City by the City'.[9] Evidence suggests that the collapse of Lehmans in 2008 did nothing to change this.[10]

Both politicians and journalists can quickly earn a reputation for sound good sense if they embrace the City orthodoxy. They also stand to make fortunes from jobs in the sector once their time in Parliament or the BBC comes to an end. If, on the other hand, they reject the City's version they may well find that they've been lumped together with the socially awkward paranoiacs that they define themselves against. The fact that socially awkward paranoiacs are often right is hardly the point. The successful are all for self-deception if knowledge leads to failure. Given this combination of incentives and threats, the witlessness of politicians looks less like a personal failing and more like a sensible career move in a structure that individuals cannot rationally hope to change.

Our current arrangements still deliver the power of decision to the same kind of people who ran things in Walter Bagehot's day (or John Locke's, come to that). But now that Parliament is no longer quite so dominated by representatives of the landed interest and their allies in metropolitan finance, elected politicians are kept daunted and at a distance from processes they are encouraged to believe are vastly complex and best left in the hands of experts, City economists, who pose as the modern equivalent of Platonic philosopher-kings.[11]

As for what Bagehot called the 'vacant many', we cannot now be satisfied with the occasional royal appearance. Told we live in a democracy, we must have an account of public life that conforms to what we are told, just as pseudo-medieval flummery once gave the peasants of Dorsetshire the sense that they lived in an unchanging monarchy. So the state has created the BBC, the most significant addition of the last century to what Paine called 'the complete organization of civil government', and therefore to what passes for the constitution, and appreciated as such by only a very few.[12]

As a national broadcaster the BBC strives to represent the spectrum of admissible opinion. This it finds in the pages of the national (that is, London) press and in the utterances of the government and its official opposition. As noted above, the City dominates discussion of economics with only rare interruptions from academics, trade unionists and backbench MPs. Meanwhile think tanks, whose funding arrangements mostly pass unmentioned, are on hand to offer more or less farcical and slanted comment on matters that the wealthy are content to manage from a distance.

Political controversy is what a handful of politicians and newspaper editors say it is. Public opinion is what a handful of popular newspapers say it is. The Corporation combines a plausible imitation of independence with loyal service to the established order and its particular patterns of silence and noise. The BBC's reproduction of this order's governing assumptions about the nature and limits of politics is all the more convincing for being largely unconscious.

The executive, and to a lesser extent the opposition, provide the focus for the broadcast media. They set the terms for what is discussed and they provide the sources of authoritative speech. For example, the Liberal Democrats lost a great deal of popular support after they entered a coalition with the Conservatives in

2010. But, as part of the executive, Liberal Democrats can now claim a share of the organized deference that the BBC affords the powerful. Decisions are made at the centre and are communicated to the concentric circles outside – from the nearby managers and influencers served by *Newsnight* to the faraway teens caught briefly by Radio 1's *Newsbeat*.

The BBC's focus on the executive and its challengers and on the content of the print media means that the audiences who pay for the BBC are quite poorly informed about matters that politicians and the print media prefer to misrepresent. Recent polling by Ipsos-Mori for Kings College London found that the public are often wildly wrong about welfare, immigration, and other contentious matters. Reflecting on the research, Martha Kearney concluded that 'I suppose we all have to get much better at talking about the real state of affairs in the country'.[13] But the job of the BBC is to reproduce the version of what's happening in the country that the executive and its opponents in Parliament have agreed to disagree about. Keenly aware of what particular demographics know, and don't know, about particular issues, politicians work with the material they have to hand, even if it means trading in fantasies. Their first concern, after all, is the temper of the people. 'The real state of affairs in the country' can take care of itself.

The BBC does not set out to discover public opinion in any systematic way, or to correct mistaken beliefs in light of the best available information. It does not seek to promote conversation between citizens who speak as equals. We have no stable ability to shape coverage or to refine our understanding through dialogue with others. The politicians are indispensable brokers in the matter of public speech. A handful of senior figures in the large parties determine the limits of the political and the BBC tailors its coverage to those limits.

The Crown-in-Parliament and its auxiliary the BBC provide invaluable resources to an effectually ruling public far smaller than the active electorate, let alone the population at large. Public opinion, in the form of data from regular polling and focus groups, provides the raw material for political messaging. It is used to develop themes in the daily 'air war' between government and opposition. The information generated remains in the hands of the political parties. The BBC meanwhile takes the print media as a proxy for public opinion and seeks to convey an account of political activity in Westminster to the public on terms largely set by the newspapers.

The notion that the BBC might host political discussion between citizens, or address matters of widespread popular confusion or ignorance, without reference to the messaging of the political parties, rarely seems to cross the minds of its journalists. The formats used to stage an ongoing national conversation prove the point. Both *Question Time* and *Any Questions* formalise the inferiority of the public relative to the professionals of speech from the major parties and from a secondary pool of the great and the good. The whole affair seems vibrant and diverse but most of what is said is said by millionaires. The public have no independent means to shape the content of the public sphere as managed by the BBC. They do not even have any secure way to discover what others think about the BBC's coverage. The data generated by the complaints procedure, which the BBC holds up as evidence of its great accountability, remains a confidential matter.

Meanwhile, scarcely one person in a hundred knows what quantitative easing is, how much the bailout cost, or how much money is spirited away by the tax avoidance business in the midst of a fiscal crisis. Most of us probably couldn't give the correct full name of the country we live in. And these extravagant failures to describe that characterise broadcast coverage of politics and the economy run alongside an infuriating professional self-confidence.

None of this is surprising. The BBC is a creature of

Parliament. It depends on Parliament for survival and cannot afford to challenge its near-monopoly on political speech. In the current climate it certainly cannot allow its coverage to reflect the stated concerns and interests of its audience in any straight-forwardly accountable way. When pushed politicians will say as much. In 2012 the former Labour Minister Gerald Kaufman was heard to declare that 'the BBC is not a democratic organization and ought not to be a democratic organization'.[14]

It is in this murk that the country's ruling public goes about its business. Their collective achievement over the last forty years is a centralised economy with high levels of inequality, in which the financial sector predominates. The changes are truly gargantuan in scale. In the 1960s finance accounted for around 2% of total profits. By 2009 the sector's share had increased by a factor of ten, to 22.5%.[15] Bank lending, the original source of much of this profitability, increased from 36.2% of GDP in 1980 to 136% of GDP in 2000. By 2008 bank lending reached 212% of GDP.[16] Private sector debt as a whole increased from 202% of GDP in 1987 to 543% of GDP in 2009.[16]

The largest three supermarket chains increased their share of the grocery market from less than 20% in the early eighties to more than 70% in the early years of this century. Their expansion has been achieved overwhelmingly at the expense of small grocery businesses.[17] New homes in Britain are, on average, the smallest in Western Europe. This, by the way, has nothing to do with living on a crowded island, as house builders and their apologists like to claim. In the Netherlands new houses are 53% larger than here, although the country is almost twice as densely populated.[18] Developers build tiny homes for their customers so that they can afford mansions for themselves. Around one in five of the UK workforce earn their living as 'guard labour' in 'security, policing, law, surveillance and forms of IT that control and monitor'. [18]

Amid all the talk of free enterprise and market forces, high incomes and status tend to accrue to those who succeed in securing access to economic rents in the public or private sectors, or in the growing grey area between the two. Politicians supplement their salaries with private lobbying work and corporate ties. According to Democratic Audit 'almost half of the UK's top firms are connected to a minister or MP'. Elsewhere, senior executives at the BBC help themselves, and each other, to extravagant multiples of the license fee in what one senior journalist has described as 'a get-rich-quick scheme'.[19] Civil servants, accountants and management consultants move in and out of government, using privileged access to policy-making to ratchet up their fees and salaries.

The template is the financial sector, where the rents derived from credit expansion are protected by a complex of legitimating narratives and an ongoing effort to corrupt and suborn threats to super-normal returns. The merger of 'utility' and 'casino' banking in the United States has attracted considerable attention, but a similar process in the UK passed mostly unremarked. The high street banks and the demutualised building societies became increasingly dependent on dealmakers from investment banking.

Those who work in finance love to complain about the amount of tax they pay, and to demand an ever more 'competitive' tax regime. But they themselves are in the business of securing tax-like revenues from people who make things and move them around the place, who care for others or entertain or educate them. John Kay, hardly a radical, is emphatic on this point:

> Everything that everyone in the City earns is ultimately money that comes from someone in the non-financial economy ... In a sense you can think of it as a tax, some of it a necessary tax, some of it an unnecessary tax, on what we call the real economy, the non-financial sector.[20]

The desire to extract the maximum possible from any revenue

stream is at the heart of the financial sector's mindset. The control it has secured over the state has therefore been disastrous. While levels of public expenditure have remained more or less stable, the amounts captured by private contractors and financiers have steadily risen. According to the International Services Group, the UK now accounts for '80 per cent of all contracting out across Europe, the Middle East, and Africa'.[21]

Attempts to assert the public interest in the face of pressure from the bankers and their allies have been dismissed as naïve, anachronistic or self-interested. A body of men (and they are mostly men) who have made money from manipulation and perception management are now at large in the state. The consequences for both morale and working conditions in the civil service have already been terrible. The same state that invented the computer and ran much of the economy with notable panache now spends fortunes on IT projects that don't work and on subsidies to privatized industry.

The current economic settlement is the creation of the executive. It was imposed on the country on the basis of nothing more than its control of a majority in Parliament. Margaret Thatcher reversed the post-war trend towards greater state ownership of industry. Telecoms, gas and electricity, water and later the railways all moved into the private sector. This generated huge fees for the bankers handling the sales and gave the City a taste for the state as profit centre. Meanwhile, her Chancellor Nigel Lawson, a former financial journalist, deregulated the City in a conscious attempt to re-establish London as the capital of global capitalism. Bankers, given their head, did what bankers like to do. They lent against property and made a fortune from the resulting bubble.

Thatcher broke the power of organized labour in order to secure what her advisor John Hoskyns called 'a sea-change in Britain's political economy'.[22] Changes to union legislation ran alongside a severe recession and steep rises in unemployment in heavily unionised sectors. The result was a secular shift in the balance of power between owners (and their financiers) on the one hand, and the wage-earning majority on the other. According to the International Labour Office, wages as a share of national income have fallen by 11.1% since the peak of the mid-seventies.[23] As the authors of that note point out, this decline takes place against a background of steeply rising pay in corporate management and in the financial sector.

When the Labour Party finally returned to office in a landslide victory in 1997 the fundamentals of the Thatcherite settlement remained in place. Indeed the new administration went further than their Conservative predecessors and gave the Bank of England control of monetary policy. In signalling their belief in Snowden's doctrine of Parliamentary incompetence Labour gained enormous credibility among those whose opinions mattered. Under Tony Blair and Gordon Brown, government left the banking sector free to increase and direct credit with little regulation or oversight. In 2006 Ed Balls, then Economic Secretary to the Treasury, told an audience of businessmen in Hong Kong that 'when the WorldCom accounting scandal broke in the US, we resisted pressures from commentators for a regulatory crackdown'. The government, he added, had 'a clear interest' in protecting 'the light touch and proportionate regulatory regime that has made London a magnet for international business'.[24]

Government didn't see finance as one interest group among others. Instead, government became a lobbyist for finance. Again in 2006, after the first meeting of the so-called 'High-Level Group', the future Prime Minister Gordon Brown told journalists that the government and the bankers were working together to 'promote the City and its financial service expertise throughout the world'.[25]

The banks took advantage of light touch regulation to lend vast amounts against commercial and residential property at home and overseas. The expansion of credit was then justified in terms of the rising asset prices it caused. The share of national income captured as financial sector profits and bonuses steadily increased. The result, as in the United States, was steepening inequality. When the resultant bubble looked set to burst in 2007-8 the Bank of England used huge amounts of public money to shore up the banks and stood by while viable businesses were starved of credit.

Throughout this period the financial sector has pursued a kind of internal, fee-based imperialism. Fund managers who are notionally responsible for much of the country's corporate sector flit from stock to stock, racking up transaction fees as they go and justifying themselves with a kind of callow callousness. Rather than presiding over companies for the long term, they are content to fleece unsuspecting customers under the cover of a largely fictitious complexity. This is hardly surprising, since they identify much more closely with investment bankers, who live near them and enjoy the same lifestyle, than with their distant clients who have much less money.[26] Native industries are starved of patient capital and forced through exhausting mergers, takeovers and private equity buyouts. Executives in non-financial companies that collaborate benefit from huge increases in pay, those who refuse find that their careers stall.

Insiders turn the savings and taxes of everyone else into commissions and then bonuses. Meanwhile the enterprises that generate the wealth grew steadily less able to fund innovation or to train skilled workers. The size and opulence of the financial sector makes no sense except to those who benefit directly. But this group dominates the state and the arterial systems of communication and prestige.

Governments take little interest in industrial development and concentrate instead on converting public revenues into corporate cash-flows through privatization, public finance initiatives, public-private partnerships, and public service reform. The state sold off natural monopolies because, in the words of one Minister, 'even where opportunities for competition are limited, there are good reasons to believe that the transfer of ownership should *of itself* produce economic benefits.'[27]

The 'good reasons' did not, of course, include evidence of any kind because there wasn't any. In fact, the evidence runs in the opposite direction. For example, the state-run East Coast mainline is 'the most efficiently run rail franchise, in terms of its reliance on taxpayer funding'.[28] On the other hand, privatization did have strongly regressive effects. National ownership after 1945 fell far short of the socialist ideal of popular oversight and control but it nevertheless secured a degree of protection for vulnerable groups. One study has estimated that a million low-income households became poorer after the selloffs of the eighties and early nineties ended cross-subsidies and cleared the way for regressive pricing of utilities.[29] The state, too, lost out as profits in the privatized companies were shielded by opaque international structures and an ingenious tax avoidance sector.

Privatization and contracting out, along with the tax avoidance business, appear to be sequels to the great agricultural enclosures of the eighteenth century. Much like the predatory arrangements in banking, fund management and property development they convert contributions from the general population into rents that in turn support an aristocratic form of life.

The domestic tilt towards finance was of a piece with the government's efforts to shore up the City's position in the global economy. In 1979 the Conservatives removed the remaining exchange controls and presided over a massive expansion of the offshore sector. Almost immediately British financiers started to create investment vehicles and trusts in low tax jurisdictions. The relative power of labour and capital began to shift in capital's favour. Since then, the state, in partnership with the City of London, has promoted finance-led globalization and acted as a faithful lieutenant of the United States. Together they sought to open up the world to the 'Anglo-Saxon' model of free trade in services and capital market liberalization. It is a model that bears a marked resemblance to British imperialism in the late nineteenth century.

Light touch regulation and a deniable network of offshore centres were used to attract newly liberated capital. Much of the money came from grand corruption and subordinate forms of organized crime like the drugs trade.[30] A balance was struck between the appearance of propriety and the reality of collusion in crime committed both offshore and at home. It is a mistake to complain about the creaking antiquity of the state system. In its adaptation to the demands of a thoroughly globalised and increasingly criminal capitalism it is in important respects the most modern on earth.

Conservative reforms in the 1980s put local government on a more or less colonial basis that devolution has only partially remedied. The conventions governing the relationship between the regions and the centre were no protection against a government determined to impose its will. In evidence to Parliament, Sir Merrick Cockell, Chairman of the Local Government Association has described England as 'the last part of the British Empire, still run, as we concede, in a way that might have worked with running India from the India Office'.[31] In many places local government has become a playground for well-connected natives working with developers and large supermarket chains. Charlie Hopkins, a solicitor in East Devon, describes the fusing of politics and business in the shires:

The further out of London you get the more like the Wild West it is. It's groups of local landowners, local gentry and local farmers. If they're not local politicians their sons are. It's not unique – it's how power works at the local level … In rural areas it is very much to do with ties to the land and connections with local politicians.[32]

A planning system that delivers windfall profits to the landed interest and ruinous patterns of development to everyone else derives from the peculiarities of the unreformed political settlement. A system of quasi-colonial administration from the centre gives oligarchic interests enormous freedom of movement in the regions. The hollowing out of local economies outside London and the return of squirearchy are political achievements that can only be remedied through changes to the general field in which politics takes place. Such changes have a direct bearing on the kinds of houses we live in, the kinds of schools our children go to and how much money we have. Yet they rarely feature in the version of the political offered us in effectually public speech.

To repeat, the domestic programme initiated under Thatcher was tied inextricably to the state's attempts to re-establish the City's position internationally. The financial oligarchy used their achievements at home as sales props in their efforts to promote similar policies overseas. Deregulation in London was of a piece with efforts to deregulate the financial sector in Europe and beyond. In 1988 the journalist William Keagan noticed that 'about a quarter of the UK delegation to the OECD Ministerial Meeting were press and propaganda officers of one sort or another'. He concluded then that 'a lot of resources' were 'being devoted to the propagation of the British Economic Miracle'.[33] Thatcher's reorganization of the domestic economy was increasingly being held up as an example for others to follow.

This push by the British state for what is euphemistically called 'trade liberalisation' continues. Peter Mandelson recently explained that the proposed EU-US trade agreement 'stands a chance of seriously advancing the frontiers of trade liberalisation and the agreements that underpin them. Success would mean 'taking an agreement way beyond the elimination of tariffs to new areas, almost virgin territory in international trade negotiation'. This in turn would present 'a real precedent and template for the rest of the international trading community'. Mandelson conceded that 'there will be some other member states who are slightly more defensive' but he insisted that 'London's approach to this is that we have to make sure the foot is kept down on the accelerator'.

A year after Keagan spotted the propagandists at the OECD, Peter Young, a researcher at the Adam Smith Institute, could be heard calling privatization 'a major British export'.[34] And the attempt to export various isotopes of privatization also continues. In 2007 the Lord Mayor of London visited India. The subsequent report noted how:

> The delegation's detailed explanations of how PPPs [public-private partnerships] have been used to enhance the development of infrastructure across a range of public services in the UK attracted a lot of interest from business and Government players, although there was much scepticism about the appropriateness of these techniques for funding the provision of social infrastructure in India's current circumstance.[35]

The report went to say that 'UK players are interested, and there is considerable business potential in advising on risk sharing and scoping of infrastructure projects – we need to press harder'.[36] Scepticism in India about the benefits of the British approach lead to calls to 'press harder'. The commission-hungry spirit of Robert Clive lives on in the offices of the Lord Mayor of London.

The empire itself, once we look pass the flags and marching bands, was a series of business models, in which profits and state support migrated from the Atlantic slave trade, to the conquest-by-privatization of India, to the predatory trade with China, mining in Southern Africa and the oil business in the Middle East and Latin America. Legitimation in the language of immemorial authority or racial superiority came later, if at all. While East India Company rule in India gave way to the Raj and the Empress Victoria, debt imperialism in South America and the

Middle East took place on an informal basis with only occasional assistance from the Royal Navy.

Once the empire is understood as a series of attempts to secure super-normal profits with the help of state power, the affinities with the contemporary settlement stand out all the more clearly. The promotion of Public-Private Partnerships echoes East India Company rule in India. HSBC established itself in the opium trade with China and later facilitated the narcotics trade between Mexico and the United States. The UK government's support for the liberalisation of trade in services and for the removal of controls on capital is of a piece with its earlier promotion of free trade and the gold standard. Both the Eurodollar market and the emerging offshore trade in the Chinese Renmimbi offer London an opportunity to retain a central position in global capital markets, a status that predates much of what we think of as the empire itself.

Modern attempts to reorganize the British state as a lobby for international finance and British itself as a testing ground for new forms of enclosure by fraud are best understood in terms of the state's lingering ambition to embody a universal mission, to exalt a particular cast of mind and with it a particular model of human flourishing. This ambition gives a mercenary character to public life. Individuals who hold their wealth offshore wield disproportionate power as funders of political parties, think tanks and academic institutions. And through the City of London the state's commitment to serve the interests of finance takes a settled institutional form with considerable powers of patronage and genteel intimidation.

British capitalism has a noticeably global perspective, through its close identification with free capital flows as well as its longstanding interest in mining and oil. This global orientation is reflected in the state's anxiety about decline and the accompanying desire to 'punch above its weight' on the world stage. Perhaps the taste for violent theatrics and the neurotic fear of decline are what all states that aspire to greatness have in common.

The virtuosity resides in both frenzied acquisition, in partnership with other winners, and suave handling of the losers. Senior managers in finance and a couple of other favoured sectors have shaped the terms on which this offshore empire has been constructed. With help from partners in Parliament, academia, and the major media these globally oriented interests have controlled the executive and its enormous powers since 1979. The absence of constitutional clarity is central to this capture of government. Constant improvisation at the centre combined with weak regional representation gives the metropolitan powers extraordinary influence over the official mind, the universities and the press.

As a matter of useful symbolism, the current Prime Minister, David Cameron, is the son of one of the pioneers in offshore investment management. Before he became leader of the Conservative Party, Cameron sat on the board of Urbium, a company that helped turn the country's high streets into factories mass producing drunk young people.[37]Cameron embodies both the offshore orientation of British financial and commercial capitalism and its degrading onshore effects.

It is not surprising that this faction has been able to capture control of policy in Britain so completely. While the executive is highly centralised and can act pretty much as it pleases between elections, finance prospers by winning the confidence of senior decision-makers in any institutional setting. It builds relationships and cultivates dependency with a single-mindedness that its rivals and opponents can rarely match. It is particularly well-suited to steeply hierarchical settings where capture of a few key decision-makers translates into enormous power.

Beset with seemingly intractable problems in the manufacturing economy, successive government have sought advice from these experts in court politics. Finance took a particularly prominent role in the restructuring of the British state after 1979. The investment bank NM Rothschild, for example, advised on the first wave of privatizations. At the onset of the most recent crisis the same bank began lobbying for schemes to extract private rents from the motorway system.[38] Investment bankers, management consultants, accountants and others regularly take jobs in key state institutions. The public sector has also been forced to adopt various forms of what Michael Sandel calls 'market-mimicking governance' that further enhance the authority of the financial sector. Of course, the financiers who have advised both Conservative and Labour governments since 1979 have had no interest in policies that would actually help the rest of the economy. Free trade, sound money and a smaller state might sound business-friendly but in the real world they are a recipe for de-industralisation.

Meanwhile, the intelligence services in Britain are lavishly funded and enjoy regular access to the Prime Minister and other senior ministers. These agencies are also active in spotting talent in the major parties and ensuring that those destined for the top jobs understand what is expected of them. According to one authoritative source 'the Anglo-Saxon model of capitalism' remains on 'MI5's list of potential targets to be safeguarded against subversion'.[39] An advocate of employee ownership and reform of the financial sector would be unlikely to make it to Downing Street without meeting fierce resistance from the defenders of a very particular kind of capitalism.

The novelist and former spy John le Carré worries that 'the secret world has become "the spiritual home" of the British political establishment, an upper clergy that is "pernicious" and "widely spread"'. His remark that 'all us have an aunt in the secret service' finds confirmation of sorts in Damian McBride's recent memoir, where he relates how his security vetting took the form of a series of intrusive questions posed to him by 'a kindly spinster aunt'.[40]

Successful politicians have tended to be enthusiastic about the agenda promoted by finance and blessed by the intelligence agencies. Financiers and intelligence officials are world-class manipulators and together they wield enormous, largely unaccountable power over both the political system and the wider climate of opinion. They have a natural affinity for one another, too. They are both in the information business, and they both prosper when they are substantially misunderstood.

The UK government's overriding need to maintain the Atlantic alliance and hence its status as a major player in global intelligence is of a piece with the Treasury-BoE-City's commitment to maintaining London's vulnerable but lucrative place in the global economy. Banks engaged in systematically criminal activity collaborate with spies who are tasked with fighting organized crime. Meanwhile the Americans have managed to hook our guardians on the inside dope, the narcotic thrill of knowing more than the French. A political culture in love with secrecy cannot bring itself to explore the implications.

By their nature politicians want to do *something* and it is all too easy to confuse what is possible with what is desirable. This comes across very strongly in Blair's case, where 'public service reform', one of the many isotopes of privatization, became an obsession once he convinced himself that active management of the economy and substantive democratization were impossible – *because they were opposed by the advocates of 'public service reform'.*

In matters both foreign and domestic the proponents of this offshore empire have dominated discussion. Often theirs are the only voices audible, since discussions that reach significant audiences usually limit themselves to differences of opinion between them. Needless to say, many of their achievements, from the first wave of privatization in the 1980s to the recent restructuring of the National Health Service, did not feature in the manifestos of the party responsible.

As in the late imperial era, the central preoccupation is with

Britain's place in world, rather than the interests of the general population. The home economy is a source of sweated profits and London is a pleasant place to live but the real action is elsewhere. Strikingly, many of the companies and individuals that together shape policy are resident but not domiciled here for tax purposes. In a submission to Parliament the City of London explained its role as a lobbyist for finance in terms that make its indifference to narrowly national considerations clear:

> *Under the City 'brand', the City of London Corporation seeks to promote and support the financial services sector in the UK regardless of the relevant home base of individual institutions, as Ambassador and facilitator for the industry irrespective of its geographical location in the UK. As such its promotional activities are not confined to the 'Square Mile' and the surrounding business cluster.*[41]

The state gives energetic diplomatic support to private companies that pay little or no tax in the UK and is currently revising the tax laws in favour of large transnational corporations. And, of course, there is also a very high level of integration with the American state. 'Anglo-Saxon capitalism' requires an Anglo-American security apparatus. Here, too, the national interest is framed in terms of a minority's global ambition for power and knowledge.

Impeccable manners run alongside an enthusiastic appetite for crime. When the financial sector reaches the limits of what can be achieved through the sharp practice its repeatedly resorts to outright criminality. Price-fixing, mis-selling and other kinds of fraud have long been a fact of life in the City of London. But the scale and frequency of the crimes have steadily increased. The manipulation of LIBOR, the most important global interest rate, is only a recent high water mark of what has been a flood of criminal behaviour since 1979. London became a place where foreign banks could pursue profits while avoiding regulation and taxation. From the Eurodollar market in the 1950s through to Enron, Party Gaming and AIG, the City has acted as a kind of offshore centre for Wall Street, a place where Americans could do things that might land them in prison back home.

From the late fifties onwards London's banks captured much the trade in dollars outside the United States, the so-called Eurodollar market. Attempts to regulate and tax capital elsewhere lent Britain a competitive advantage that has been obscured by talk of time zones and humanity's propensity to truck, barter and exchange. It is in this light that we should understand George Osborne's stated ambition 'to make London a western hub' for the offshore trade in China's currency.[42]

Together with a clutch of overseas territories and Crown dependencies the City of London forms a labyrinth of unreformed jurisdictions that achieve a state of wave-particle ambiguity, at once reassuringly British and inviolately offshore. It now offers the rest of the world a dependable and gentlemanly respite from the hurly burly of accumulation at gunpoint. Where better to stash the proceeds of crime than here, in the much-misunderstood Roman heart of a magical kingdom? So marginal anomalies – quirky incidentals in our island story – have become central to the operations of the global economy.

The City of London uses its dual status as local authority and financial lobby to promote the interests of the financial sector in the state, in civil society, and overseas. The intelligence establishment understands subversion in terms of threats to these same interests. The Bank of England wields enormous power that escapes general comprehension, never mind democratic control. In each instance a sophisticated information economy shaped by legislation and state provision 'ordains which of the sciences should be studied in a state, and which each class of citizens should learn, and up to what point they should learn them'.[43]

This careful control of knowledge extends to the state's published account of itself. *The Cabinet Manual*, which the Chairman of the Commons' Political and Constitutional Reform Committee, Graham Allen MP, called 'the closest thing we have to a written constitution', makes the point eloquently.[44] Though it claims to set out 'the conventions determining how the Government operates', the *Manual* finds no room to set out the constitutional status of the City of London, the intelligence agencies, the Bank of England, or the BBC.

Many members of the groups that together control the executive are the products of the same schools and universities. But it is important to grasp that, in Anthony Barnett's words, 'it is not the strength of the public schools and Oxford/Cambridge that sustains the existing order of the constitution. The constitution sustains its feeder institutions'.[45] The mix of national and international projects described above favours particular attitudes and habits of mind and certain conceptions of the self. Though they can be found in anyone, they are deliberately encouraged by certain kinds of upbringing.

The public schools introduce those they teach to a daylight of rule-based hierarchy and a night-time in which other considerations prevail. The teachers inveigh against the same abuses that ensure stability. In due course high spirits are forgiven and bullies become prefects. Those educated in such conditions become keenly aware of the difference between public declarations and private understandings. This emphasis on hierarchy and hypocrisy against a gothic backdrop provides an excellent preparation for life in the country's uncodified, and encoded, public life. It is for this reason above all that the schools secure disproportionate representation for their pupils in the ancient universities, and then the higher reaches of finance and politics – they prepare their charges for the world that exists.

Eton in particular has enjoyed spectacular success in recent years, but more generally the large non-state sector trains a minority in a way that marks them out from the majority and estranges them from their contemporaries. Imperialism in one country is that much easier when its administrators enjoy a degree of social distance from those who are to be administered. This perhaps also goes some way to explaining the success of the British in advertising and public relations. Manipulation through charm and genteel intimidation comes easily to the products of such a background.

Meanwhile, the education provided by the state offers little in the way of an introduction to the structure of the governing institutions, or to the habits and assumptions that underpin them. By the time they leave school most people are still very far from understanding what to a few has become second nature. The choice appears to be between withdrawal from political action or energetic imitation of those who already understand how the game is played.

Only a few are explicitly educated in the character of the public world. The rest must learn later by observation, trial and error. But it is still true, as in Earl John Russell's time, that 'the democratic character of the nobility, the democracy of the aristocracy if I may be allowed to call it, is very much to be attributed to the gregarious education they receive. In this manner, her public schools form a part of the constitution of the country'.[46] Public schools ensure that the wealthy do not become hopelessly isolated from the rest of society. They provide a venue in which much of the next generation of national leaders learns to cooperate and compete with one another. Privilege and talent mix in a giddy and indecipherable combination. Those who succeed have the self-confidence that comes from knowing that some who enjoyed the same advantages have failed.

It is simply not true that the unreformed and unexamined settlement doesn't really matter, as its more serpentine defenders like to insist. It has important consequences for the distribution of knowledge, wealth and power, both here and throughout the global system. The current arrangements are obscure to most people, but they are hospitable to those whose interests usually prevail. Indeed, their obscurity is part of how business is done. In the words of William Blackstone, Parliament 'can, in short, do every thing that is not naturally impossible'. But there are important, and useful, limits even here, where our arrangements appear most clear-cut. The House of Commons only acts where the Crown's sovereign authority is already established. Inasmuch as the City of London preserved its liberties under the kings it retains them to this day. The extent of the City's independence is, like that of the Crown dependencies, a matter of straight-faced make-believe that leaves the financial sector in substantial control. The people of London vote for a Mayor who does not administer the capital's ancient centre, the City of London itself.

Note again how the absence of explicit checks and balances allows for considerable flexibility. Constitutional propriety becomes a matter of what the country's rulers can get away with at a given moment. Legality itself remains firmly in the hands of the executive through its control of Parliament. Meanwhile, the police, the prosecuting authorities and the courts are guided by a conception of the public interest that combines exemplary sentences for rioting welfare claimants with torpor in the face of elite criminality. The fusion of the executive and the legislature provides the background conditions for the fusion of the state and the financial sector and for the fusion of the police with organized crime.

In such circumstances, the majority have been powerless to prevent reckless incompetence and much, much worse. So long as the culprits acknowledge the paramount shared interests of those who dominate public life, they are free to exercise what Rupert Murdoch memorably called their 'little smidgeon of power'. The mystery in Westminster presides over countless subsidiaries of smug impunity and outright abuse. This political settlement of ours – Burke's traditional constitution – is a composite of warm bodies and cold calculation. It is manipulative to its marrow and the magic worked on the electorate finds its parallel in the magic worked on individuals in hospitals and care homes. We know little about those who occupy privileged positions in British institutions. Sometimes something monstrous is glimpsed through the mists of shared complicity. Much, including the means by which a little becomes visible, remains obscure. But this much is clear, at least some of our rulers are the stuff of nightmares.

The current arrangements contain both monarchical and anti-monarchical elements. Like any stable system it has sufficient flexibility to permit fierce competition within agreed limits. Sincere friends of the Palace like David Cameron must find an accommodation with News International, which has specialised in promoting Nixonian resentment about the shortcomings of the established order to which it belongs and over which it has exercised considerable influence. Popular curiosity is a significant profit centre and popular sentiment carries a great deal of weight in the game of consensual elite rule. But there are lines that cannot be crossed. The royal correspondent at the *News of the World*, Clive Goodman, went to prison along with Glenn Mulcaire in 2007, having been found guilty of accessing the voicemail messages of Princes William and Harry. Other victims of surveillance have had to wait much longer to be acknowledged.

While there is room for anti-monarchism, personal ambition is usually better served by properly nuanced acceptance of the established order. In this way energy and ambition are not stifled but integrated with the energy and ambition of the offshore empire. Of course, egalitarian democracy is unwelcome on all sides, offending as it does both the liberal and the conservative styles of command. Most serious players prefer to enjoy the subtleties of an unreformed system that is also a place to live, a shared irony, a game of recognition that is both deadly serious and great fun. Styles of speech and of handshake, habits of deference and command, and the maintenance of stable patterns of controversy help articulate the famously obscure rules. It has something to offer both the brilliant adventurer and the dependable creature of habit. Somewhere near the centre is the Crown, unimportant ornament and unmoved mover of the sovereign power.

The fact that power formally derives from the Crown tells the majority that constitutional arrangements don't *really* matter, because, after all, Britain is a democracy. A minority learn, to the contrary, that they matter a very great deal. The absence of formal popular sovereignty is part of how the puzzle of elite control in Britain is solved. It is not enough that those who dominate get what they want. They must do so with every appearance of propriety. Their radical innovations must seem like the outcome of natural processes or the culmination of a millennial island story.

This could now end. One by one our major institutions have broken out in a fever of revelations. The City of London, Parliament, News International, the police, the BBC … Each revelation matters because it gives comprehensible expression to a broader failure to act in the general interest. Money laundering and fraud in the City are of a piece with the sector's disastrous pre-eminence in economic management. The MPs and their expenses claims embody Parliament's surrender to the City orthodoxy. Criminal conspiracy in the media relates to a wider inability to describe the shared world. State authority, in Burke's account, is personal virtue amplified. But this embodiment of power is now undermining the governing settlement, as individual derelictions make the structure's shortcomings all the more vividly detestable.

An effort to end these abuses does not have to choose between dazed indifference to the constitution and frantic anti-monarchism. If the people wish to retain a crowned head of state, then why should we not? In his discussion of Rome's transformation from kingdom to republic, Machiavelli recommended that reform to establish 'a new and free way of life' retain 'as much of the ancient ways as possible'. It is those who want to establish a tyranny that 'must create everything anew'.[48]

Even Athens, the prototype of radical democracy, kept some elements of its ancestral constitution. The Eupatrid clan, which once dominated government, retained hereditary responsibilities relating to purification from the guilt of murder. Do we prefer a substantially reformed, albeit crowned, constitution or a more perfect oligarchy concealed and protected by a republican façade? If we want to secure something without precedent, a large egalitarian republic, a little bit of tradition seems a small price to pay.[49] Besides, reform that satisfies itself with merely 'secularising oligarchic power', in Hilary Wainwright's phrase, is unlikely to appeal to a large constituency.[50]

Most of us think we live in a democracy that is also a constitutional monarchy. We do not, and it is time we did. Republican reform, insofar as it concerns itself with the status of the monarchy, need only ask that the forms of the constitution be altered to set them in line with what we think they are already. That is the essence of a change that is necessary and desirable and that presents no challenge to the existing structures of sentiment. Its achievement would be a minor alteration that would also mark the beginning of a revolution in British affairs.

For a constitution establishing popular sovereignty cannot be granted by the Crown-in-Parliament. Those, like Stephen Haseler, who think that 'a new republican doctrine could be enacted quite simply: by an Act of Parliament designating the Speaker of the House of Commons as the Head of State' have not entirely grasped what republicanism is.[51] Popular sovereignty, as the basis of all lawful authority, must be prior to any and all institutional features of the state, including both Crown and Parliament. It cannot be secured by a mere act of Parliament. The establishment of a normal monarchy carries a charge that will explode the pretensions of Parliament. For it can only be established by means of a generally recognised constitutional convention.

The campaign for Scottish independence makes the supporters of the Westminster system nervous for many reasons. But one of them is the model it provides the rest of the UK. The Northern Irish, Cornish, Welsh and English might follow the Scots and seek to deprive the old order of its population to command. After such a process of independence the people, not Parliament, will be, in Henry Parker's phrase, 'the fountaine and efficient cause' of power.[52]

The formal assertion of popular sovereignty will be very soon become vacuous, however, if it is not part of a wider process of democratization that reaches far beyond the Crown-in-Parliament to embrace the institutions of communication, subsidy and credit. Without this wider programme, the offshore empire will adapt itself to the new conditions, create new structures of sentiment and new orthodoxies of thought. Ways will be found to ensure that a formally sovereign people remain confused and disconcerted.

The aim of republicanism is to give substantial, as well as formal power, to the citizen body, such that each citizen has an equal voice in government, an equal share of the state. Only this public liberty will enable us to protect ourselves from arbitrary power in the form of force or fraud. The next two chapters describe first republicanism as a body of thought and second the outlines of a maximally republican constitution.

Chapter 3

Republican Principles

If there is a surplus of good, it resides in the people
Niccolò Machiavelli

A republic exists when the state is the shared possession of a sovereign public. In Cicero's words 'respublica [est] res populi' – 'the republic belongs to the people'. In a democratic republic the entire adult population formally holds an equal share in this state as property held in common. In modern times possession has usually been codified in a written constitution. A maximally republican system is designed to ensure that the adult population has the means to make good on its formal ownership of the state. The state takes the form the population prescribes and does what the population directs. As we shall see this means revising what we mean by a constitution.

The state-owning and sovereign public recognises no authority higher than itself and permits no external restraints on its actions. It is at liberty to assert its will in all matters pertaining to its interests. It must impose limits on this liberty, in the form of a Bill of Rights, say, or a separation of powers. Indeed, a population becomes a public when it submits to certain restrictions, including the rule of law. Its survival as a public depends on its ability to respect limits to individual and collective liberty. But people cannot absent themselves permanently from any element of the constitution – any law, regulation, custom or precedent – to which it submits. In the end the sovereign power must include the liberty to remove all restrictions.

Each citizen understands the rules that apply to them and has an equal capacity to call these rules into question. Both the law and its execution are subject to review and reform in accordance with principles that are themselves subject to review and reform. Equal subjection to the law runs alongside equal control over the law.

The public liberty to shape and direct the state is not the same as freedom in the casual sense of the word. When we normally talk about freedom we talk about doing as we please. But public liberty is a power to challenge the whole content of our shared arrangements and to combine with others to change it. The inhabitants of any nation can be free in the first sense, if they happen to be left alone in their ordinary business.

Most people are free only within quite narrow constraints. Wage-earners stand in a condition of structural dependence on employers that sometimes leaves them free during the evening and at weekends, but increasingly does not. Only those who have achieved full citizenship in a republic are free in the sense that they collectively possess, and hence have the power to direct, or frustrate, the coercive potential of the state and of their fellow citizens. They do not submit to any power of which they do not approve or which they cannot annul.

Personal freedom can only be secure when each of us holds an inalienable share of the state's power. In the words of Abraham Lincoln, 'allow all the governed an equal voice in the government and that, and that only is self-government'.[1] Possession of the state by all citizens has important consequences for the whole of a society and for the individuals within it. Institutions subordinate to the state are all subject to revision by an invigilating public. A sovereign public can dismantle structures it does not like and crush powers it decides are illegitimate. At the same time, no one is helpless in the face of arbitrary interference. Everyone can proceed in her or his endeavours without the prospect of such interference.

Public liberty does not rely on the good character of rulers, the goodwill of officials, or the forbearance of employers and magnates. It is sustained through a permanent effort of mutual surveillance. Though the majority will find many reasons to limit the freedom of minorities or to harass individuals it finds troublesome, it has one excellent reason not to. As Eleanor Roosevelt pointed out, 'if you curtail what the other fellow says or does, you curtail what you yourself may say or do'.[2] Abstract universal rights have the protection of flesh and blood citizens, who seek to secure their own continued liberty through the assertion of those rights. Restraints on any fraction of the public are evidence of a failure of public reason that most citizens have good reason to remedy.

The survival of an egalitarian, democracy republic depends on the citizen body remaining united and rejecting attempts to disqualify individuals from claiming some share of ownership in the state through fictitious distinctions based on birth, possessions, race or sex. In this sense democratic has an inescapably republican character. If any category of person can be deprived of public status on arbitrary grounds, then no category is safe. We are left with a scramble for security, where only the cunning and the ruthless have any grounds for confidence.

The essentials of this are so well understood in the ruling class as to go largely unremarked. After all, shared possession of the state is what defines a ruling class. The current arrangements in Britain can best be understood as an occult republic, in which a tightly circumscribed group operate as a public in a manner that is radically under-publicised. But there is no law of nature that decrees that the state-possessing public – the body politic – cannot consist of the entire adult population. Every claim to special virtue on the part of rulers has been disproved, as has every allegation of general incapacity. Prejudice against universal public status survives because it is vital to those who currently rule.

The most striking feature of modern politics has been the preservation of steep political inequality in conditions of formal democracy. A coalition of the wealthy and the politically astute

has achieved this by accepting the need for paradox and cooper-
ating as a secret public. In this way a few men have kept effective
ownership of the state in their own hands, even if they have had
to pretend that they were helpless to resist market forces or the
dictates of rational administration. They have achieved their
exaltation by selling a chain of pretended necessities to everyone
else under such swindling names as war, competition and nature.

Republicanism in the sense of shared ownership of the state
has something in common with anarchism. For to own a thing is
to claim the right to remake it. I do not fully own what I am not
free to destroy. The anarchist might want to say that ownership
in this strong sense is indefensible, except insofar as it relates to
the state. But, if they truly desire the destruction of the state in its
current form, anarchists will want to own it first. Republicanism
furnishes the means to achieve anarchism. For a sovereign people
is free to diminish the scope of state action, change its nature, or
replace it with a federation of self-governing communities. And it
can do so in the daylight of democratic legitimacy, where all
prudent anarchists will want to remain, given what waits for
them in the dark.

Similarly, socialism without republicanism will soon degenerate into a swindle, since those best able to mobilise class
sentiment are not necessarily most inclined to create a socialist
society. Fraternity without equality in liberty is a recipe for
betrayal. But general participation and oversight of the state will
allow citizens to discover for themselves how they wish to
reconcile private property and the public good.

One thing is clear, the sovereign public of a democratic
republic must assert itself over and above the claims of private
property. Those who believe in the perfect inviolacy of private
property cannot reconcile this belief with republicanism as rule
by the population as a whole. Capitalism is a system in which
concentrations of private property, in partnership with the state,
effectively determine the nature of social and economic devel-

opment. As such, capitalism rejects the principle of equality between citizens and sets itself against the idea that all adults possess an equal share in the sovereign power. Capitalism in this sense is therefore inconsistent with a maximally republican constitution.

Full-blooded republicanism is wary of markets since market actors can never be trusted to limit themselves to lawful competition in markets. If individuals and organizations *can* reach beyond the market to suborn the state and the institutions of civil society, and if doing so confers advantage, competitive pressure will make it likely that they will do so. Successful companies and individuals will tend therefore to make alliances with the state and other institutions, including those that seek to regiment the beliefs of others, in order to convert revenues into rents and so make their success more durable and the failure of their rivals more certain. Competition in markets makes whatever is possible necessary, including bribery, fraud, theft and murder. The trend – clearly observable in Britain – is towards ever more complete criminality against a background of intellectual collapse.

Consider finance and the discipline of economics. A lobby for radical deregulation flattered and bribed a social science until it became its reliable auxiliary. Now enormous sums are spent covering up crimes with reassuring euphemisms while the wrong-headed remain infuriatingly self-assured. The coverage of the sector is so marbled with undeclared threats and incentives that those whose errors are useful to finance enjoy professional advancement and prestige while those who are substantially correct must exhaust themselves stating the obvious to audiences who cannot help but see them as a shabby and disreputable fringe. Rarely has vice been so handsomely rewarded, or virtue so consistently punished, as in this country here and now.

Consider, too, the pharmaceutical sector and the life sciences. Massive profits paid for the wholesale corruption of understanding. Scientists and journalists noisily defended rationality while they popularised myths cooked up by marketing executives. The business needs of pharmaceutical companies, rather than the dictates of reason and evidence, have shaped the treatment of generations of people suffering from physical disease and mental distress. Public subsidies poured into the private sector where they went to support lines of research that promised to generate lucrative patents. Those who could speak authoritatively were bribed or bullied into line. Once again the result has been a kind of enclosure, this time of knowledge. Intellectual property indeed.

Consider the administration of government, where, under the rubric of 'new public management' performance-related pay, internal 'markets', and targets weakened and then displaced the ethos of public service. Elected politicians began to sound more and more like graduate trainees. Here's Peter Mandelson expressing the spirit of the age:

> *It has been the job of New Labour's architects to translate their understanding of the customer into offerings he or she is willing to pay for. And then, and only then, to convey to potential customers the attributes of that offering though all the different components that make up a successful brand – product positioning, packaging, advertising and communications.*[3]

In the midst of all this excitement it is hardly surprising that MPs began to see their expenses as profit centres, or that government began to identify exclusively with the interests of a handful of people in a handful of business sectors.

Many of the partisans for successful market actors were effective precisely because they thought they were independent. Modern courts teem with oblivious courtiers. Consider, though, News International and its dual pursuit of a political edge and commercial advantage. Here the game was played with a little more self-awareness. One of its newspapers, the *News of the World*, was spying on politicians, while another, *The Times*, was telling them what to do in elegant editorials.

Republicanism must oppose capitalism insofar as it must oppose anything that threatens popular sovereignty. But while republicanism in a strong sense implies deep suspicion of private property and market exchange, it does not necessarily imply hostility. A sovereign people can treat private property and free exchange as two goods among many or it can tolerate them as necessary evils. It can decide that they are no longer needed and sweep them away. But it cannot accept them as equals, much less as superiors. The claim that property somehow stands above politics is absurd in fact and disgusting in its implications. But to establish the primacy of the sovereign public over property has serious implications for Britain's economic settlement, which rests precisely on its promise to protect private wealth, and to elevate it above the claims of democracy. Once one strips away the evasive language this promise to property is the key to understanding both domestic and foreign policy in Britain.

The public that owned the ancient and renaissance state was not a public that most of us would now recognise as such. When Cicero wrote, it was self-evident that only free adult males were capable of any kind of public status. And only a small minority of those could be trusted to execute important public business. A few families controlled most of the elective offices, even if talented outsiders like Cicero himself could occasionally break into the celebrity of excellence that the Romans called nobility. In other ancient republics only those who owned land – or suffi-cient wealth to pay for military kit – qualified for full citizenship. Athens was unusual, if not quite unique, in permitting landless men to vote in the assemblies, an innovation they themselves called *isonomia* and that their scandalised enemies called *democrasia*.[4]

More fundamentally, the ancient and early modern models

for republican government excluded most of the adult population. Women and slaves were not permitted a public status. Indeed, the exclusion of women is integral to the classical idea of constitutional government. In the Greek imagination despotism was characterised by the overt or covert power of women. The all-male assembly was a brightly lit rejection of the King's palace, a half-dark where pleasure mingled with tyranny. Athenian women who appeared in the open air did so veiled. In the so-called golden age of democracy the streets of Athens would have looked much more like modern Riyadh than, say, Athens.

It is tempting to conclude that the brutality and misogyny of ancient and not so ancient republics disqualify them as objects of interest, much less of emulation. Why should we care how racist and sexist warmongers in ancient Rome organized their affairs? But the enemies of popular emancipation have no such reservations about the republican past. They understand full well that their power and liberty depend on their effective control of the state. Indeed, it is their permanent ambition to act as a sovereign public in the classical sense. The state is an instrument for their enrichment, of course. But more than that it is the guarantor of their dignity, the assistant to their plans, the venue for their, necessarily constrained, celebrity. They make the state an instrument for frustrating popular interests and projects, for bewildering their enemies, for giving their own wishes the force of law, for dignifying their crimes, and prettifying their vices. The state's limitlessness reflects their ambitions. Its power to seize wealth gives them what little sense of security they have, since as Machiavelli notes, 'men do not believe they truly possess what they own, if they do not acquire still more from others'.[5] The state is the means by which these few savour something of the divine, in what one historian has called the 'conscious mastery of men and events'.[6]

But, to repeat, these modern day inheritors of classical republicanism cannot declare themselves. Their triumphs can never be described openly as such. They prosper only if they are misunderstood. By contrast, those of us who choose to renovate republican ideals and put them at the service of general liberation enjoy an incalculable advantage. We can act in the open, without the nods and winks of the boardroom and the working breakfast. The frank language of liberty and power, of liberty-as-power, is ours for the taking.

Those who suffer abuse and violence in the current political settlement can only expect an end to their ill treatment when they have claimed their proper share of state power, and so broken the exclusive claims of their enemies. The insider – the politician, the plutocrat, the fixer – who hates the ordinary run of ordinarily distracted humanity comforts himself with the thought that this great majority will never discover itself as the rightful possessor of state power. He feels sure that some expedient will always present itself as a serviceable distraction. He is more than happy that the possibilities of republicanism remain obscure, that it is confused with something else. If women and men without property remain estranged from republican doctrines then the unprincipled and indefensible public that exerts effective control over the state, over the distribution of private and public goods and over the climate of opinion, will remain undisturbed.

The democratic-republican rejection of racism and sexism does not rest on any special tenderness towards those harassed and harmed. It rests instead on the commitment to equal ownership of the state. Once we accept that we are all muddle-headed and clear-sighted, self-interested and selfless, rational and irrational, and that we all have a claim to public status, then prejudice against one is a threat to all. And we can discard all the incidentals of classical republicanism, so long as we grasp the central point: individual liberty cannot survive without collective ownership of the state.

The original republics were small. Classical Athens was little bigger than a modern town. Two thousand years later, the republics of renaissance Italy struggled to expand beyond their origins as the governments of walled cities. When America rebelled against the British Crown it was a patchwork of self-governing communities that were, for the most part, little bigger than classical Athens. The exchange economy was smaller, too. Most households were much closer to self-sufficiency than they are now.

The exclusion of women, slaves and men without property further limited the size of the political nation.[7] The citizens of the classical republics knew one another and knew their elected officials. The normal business of life brought citizens much of the political information that they needed. Barbershops in Athens were notorious haunts for amateur experts in foreign policy. And what the citizen missed in the daily round could be supplied in face-to-face assemblies and through direct participation in government. It is in the assembly above all that the citizens discovered themselves as a body politic. Expansion was the enemy of republican rule. The constitutions of the Roman and Venetian republics became more and more fictitious as the cities became imperial powers.

Modern states are much larger and more complex. They have not always descended into Caesarism or abject oligarchy. But neither have they solved the problems that arise when everyday life no longer furnishes the necessities of political information. At present constitutional government is being subverted by those who hold privileged positions in the institutions of communication, credit and intelligence. Whether we call them an aristocracy of knowledge or a manipulative cabal, these few labour to shape public opinion, in order to rule in its name. The story they are avid to tell is of a people too selfish, too stupid, or too vicious for the demands of self-government.

One response to the problem of scale, now associated with

strict interpretations of the United States constitution, has been to call for a radical simplification and diminution of the state. The great glory of this tradition has been its recognition of the threat war poses to republican government. War demands unquestioning loyalty to the nation while the survival of the republic requires constant suspicion of the state. War is a kind of artificial complexity, an invented zone of secrecy and unreason that defies popular oversight and control. In America it has become the favoured means politicians use to escape the indignities and uncertainties of democracy.

Conventional wars, ostensibly in the service of oppressed humanity or humane principle, have been supplemented by frozen confrontation with the Soviet Union and by the War on Drugs. Once the Soviet menace could no longer serve the required purpose. The second President Bush bodged together themes from a series of more or less fantastical conflicts to concoct a War on Terror. All this, it now seems clear, was part of a process by which war and the threat of war first deprived the population of its status as a public and then progressively inured them to the experience of passivity.[8]

But there is another response to the problem of scale. Instead of weakening and simplifying the state it proposes to strengthen and complicate the public. The state becomes subject to effective oversight and control by a sovereign public. The propertied and ambitious few do not capture the state while dividing and confusing everyone else. All pretexts for privilege – from special talent to the monstrous expedient of war – are exposed to constant rational test. This is preferable, insofar as it supports the provision of public goods through the state, while preventing the forms of constitutional government from becoming a cover for unaccountable and unacknowledged interests – instead of a minimal government, a maximum republic.[9]

The new digital technologies make this idea of an enriched, informed and emboldened public easier to imagine. There is no need for utopianism about the potential of the networked society. We can already see how information stored online combined with social media can support sophisticated debate and deliberation. It is crucial, however, that we grasp the implications of these new technologies for constitutional design. Dick Costolo, the CEO of Twitter, articulates a commonly held delusion among billionaires that we can create a 'global town square' that will contain, rather than be contained by, politicians and their adjutants in the private economy:

> … *if you went back to Ancient Greece, the way that news and information was passed around was, you went to the Agora after lunch in the town square. I might go to the Agora and say to Martin, 'Hey my aunt died'. There was this unfiltered, multi-directional exchange of information. Martin might say 'Euripides' goat passed away'. By the way, the politicians were there. The musicians were there, et cetera. There was this multi-directional, unfiltered exchange of information that was interesting in all sorts of ways.*[10]

The revelations about NSA and GCHQ surveillance only made explicit what should have been obvious to anyone capable of reasoning from first principles. The state will seek to maintain order by monitoring the 'multi-directional, unfiltered exchange of information' and using overt or covert means to ensure that it retains the capacity to both filter and direct conversation in the global (and national) town squares. The new technologies are being embedded in frameworks of law and customary practice. They are subject to all manner of interference by economic and political power. They will be made to serve the logics of information dominance and profit maximisation if we do not act to make them the instruments of a sovereign public.[11]

The remedy for current and future abuses is to be found in a renewed application of republican principles to changed conditions. We agree with the principled opponents of government in their hatred of war as an instrument of criminal acquisition and domination at home as well as abroad. But the circumstances in which we find ourselves, and the resources with which we have to work, have changed since the early days of the American republic. Those of us who argue for a revived republicanism do not think that private property is God given and somehow prior to the state, any more than we think that money must be backed by gold. Instead we desire to increase the scope of popular engagement in the workings of a large and complex state to ensure that everything, including property, is understood and respected on terms that are just and durable.

In the modern age even a radically simplified state will far outstrip the unaided understanding of the individual citizen. The growth of the political nation has reduced the relative importance of face-to-face communication. Daily life no longer gives us the information we need in order to exercise independent political judgement. Walter Lippmann thought that what he called 'spontaneous democracy' depends on conditions that 'approximate those of the isolated rural township'.[12] We therefore rely on the media to tell us about the faraway world where many decisions that affect us take place. The mass media, and the technologies that underpin them, have become matters of deep constitutional significance, even if they do not feature much in our constitutional thought.[13]

This near silence about the relationship between power and knowledge stands in marked contrast with classical political philosophy, which was preoccupied by the question of who learns what and how. As already noted, at the beginning of the *Ethics*, Aristotle explains that politics 'ordains which of the sciences should be studied in a state, and which each class of citizens should learn, and up to what point they should learn them'.[14] The later era of constitution-building in the eighteenth century also paid attention to the question of information. The American constitution, for example, makes some provision to ensure the circulation of ideas without state interference.

Article 1 states that 'Congress shall make no law respecting an establishment of religion, or prohibiting the free exercise thereof; or abridging the freedom of speech, or of the press; or the right of the people peaceably to assemble, and to petition the Government for a redress of grievances'. But mass education, broadcast and now digital technologies have supplemented the printed press and radically altered what each class of citizen can expect to learn. If we are to write a constitution in Britain then it will need to take these changes in the field of communications into account.

Attempts to distribute power equally that do not ensure an even distribution of relevant knowledge are bound to be frustrated. As Aristotle well knew, unequal access to knowledge helps preserve and protect other forms of inequality. The systems of communication in the broadest sense – the traditional media, the digital media, the schools and libraries – cannot be left beyond the reach of a people that wishes to be, and remain, sovereign. This is not to argue for state ownership of the media. Rather, republican rule depends on a rough equality in the power to describe reality, and to bring relevant descriptions to the attention of fellow citizens. The mass media currently have a unique power to describe themselves and to frame the controversies that surround, and confound, us all. They can decide what to notice and what to ignore, as long as they do not irritate those with the power to do them harm. Given that they are not accountable to the wide public, it is to be expected that they will betray that wide public, while insisting on their good faith. And this is what we repeatedly find.

While the ancient republics neurotically suppressed non-citizens, the citizens themselves had to be more or less equal in economic terms since civic equality depended on this parity of material possession. Later republicans also understood this. For in steeply unequal societies the poor will end up doing the bidding of the rich. As the English republican James Harrington put it during the revolutionary wars of the seventeenth century, 'he who wants bread is his servant that will feed him'.[15]

For Harrington, the distribution of land determined the form of government. If one man owned the land, there would be absolute monarchy. If a few people owned the land there would be limited monarchy. Only if the whole people were landlords could a commonwealth survive: 'where there is inequality of estate there must be inequality of power, and where there is inequality of power, there can be no commonwealth'. Therefore at the heart of his republican programme was a law enforcing the necessary equality of estate, and so preventing a small number of landowners from subverting the republic:

> An equal agrarian is a perpetual law, establishing and preserving the balance of dominion by such a distribution, that no man or number of men within the compass of the few or the aristocracy, can come to overpower the whole people by their possession in lands.[16]

A century later the American revolutionaries were well aware of the relationship between economic and political equality and some of them at least wrote in terms that recall Harrington's insistence on the need for 'equality of estate'. Noah Webster argued in 1787 that:

> An equality of property, with a necessity of alienation, constantly operating to destroy combinations of powerful families, is the very soul of a republic – While this continues, the people will inevitably possess both power and freedom; when this is lost, power departs, liberty expires, and a commonwealth will inevitably assume some other form.[17]

More than a century later the connections between property, liberty and power could still occasionally break into the political mainstream in America. The Populists' Omaha Platform of 1892 complained that 'from the same prolific womb of governmental injustice we breed two great classes – tramps and millionaires'.[18] It was understood that state power determined the distribution of property and, at the same time, that the distribution of property determined the true nature of the state. A generation after the Populists, the future Supreme Court Justice Louis Brandeis remarked that 'we may have democracy in this country or we may have wealth concentrated in the hands of a few, but we can't have both'.[19]

As new sources of wealth were discovered, and new instruments for its concentration were devised in the period after the Civil War, the American state faced the prospect of transformation. By the end of the twentieth century this transformation was all but complete. Warnings like those of Brandeis and the Populists were being drowned in a molasses of soothing reassurance. In 1996 the President Bill Clinton insisted that 'we are not a people who object to others being successful, we do not resent people amassing their own wealth fairly won in the free enterprise system'.[20]

When Clinton spoke he knew full well that the free enterprise system had long been destroyed and replaced by industrial, agricultural, and above all financial, combinations. Inequality grew even steeper under Clinton than it had been under Reagan and Bush. Yet an equality of property was no longer, as in Webster's definition, 'the soul of a republic'. In fact, according to the President it was somehow un-American. Clinton's enduring popularity is, I am afraid, evidence that the commonwealth there has taken on a new form.

The great fortunes in America in modern times have been made through speculation in corrupt financial markets, through preferential access to credit, and through the appropriation of state revenues, most notably in the arms industry. Meanwhile a handful of beneficiaries of public investments in information technology – Bill Gates, Steve Jobs, Eric Schmidt – have lent a shallow plausibility to the lie that the free enterprise system killed by industrial and financial consolidation a century ago still survives.

A renovated republicanism will, like its predecessors, address land ownership. But it will also look carefully at the rest of the economy. The restoration of the small and middling farmer, however desirable, would leave the majority unaffected. Most of us sell our labour for wages, which we use to pay for everyday necessities and to service the interest on debts. The wage relation and the need to secure credit from private banks undermine the independence of the citizen. We must do what we are told at work. Increasingly we must believe what we are told, if we are to do what is required of us and remain reasonably content. It is painful to admit that we are not free. Meanwhile, distress and danger accompany any stirrings of republican sentiment. And employers do not like workers who aspire to civic equality. They prefer those who know their place, who look upwards for any improvement in their condition, not sideways to their fellow workers, who are also fellow citizens. We are frightened of being made redundant ('let go' in the inadvertently revealing euphemism), and enticed by the consolations of submission.

An effective republican programme now must encompass both the structure of the enterprise and the systems of credit. Citizens must be free to meet and speak as equals about matters that concern them. As long as we are vulnerable to punishment by employers, or susceptible to the rewards they can offer in exchange for obedience, we will be incapable of both candour and the energy of thought that derives from the free exchange of opinions. Power relations in the corporate economy are incompatible with our independence. So they must be replaced with forms of employment that safeguard the freedom of the individual to help determine the nature of his or her shared conditions. The argument against the corporation is not primarily economic. Even if corporations were more efficient than the alternatives – and they are not – the republic cannot tolerate the threat they pose to an independent citizenry.

Almost all the money in circulation is created by commercial banks in the form of debt. Hence the distribution of demand in the economy is determined by private organizations. Not surprisingly, insiders help themselves to much of the purchasing power thus created. Here again, something like enclosure takes place. The credit-worthiness of the country as a whole provides rents to a favoured few.

When banks lend to excess and in the wrong sectors, disaster looms and central banks rush to save them. The rest of the population ends up underwriting their losses. At every turn state power is used to maintain and increase the wealth of bankers and their favoured clients, who then buy further privileges from the state and fund far-reaching propaganda campaigns. In a republic the creation of money, an essentially political matter, cannot be left in private or secret hands. Credit creation is a means by which we can improve our public and private circumstances. Like land, knowledge, and other 'means of being usefully industrious' it is, in John Thelwall's phrase, 'the common right of all'.[21]

Ownership of anything is vacuous if others can tell you how you are to use it, or can deprive you of knowledge of its nature. Possession without knowledge is a prequel to successful fraud. Independence requires freedom from the exercise of arbitrary power, including the power of employers, investors and financiers. It also requires the power to inquire into, and to discuss the status of, publicly relevant information. While there may never be any final facts of the matter, accounts that can bear sustained public scrutiny are the only reasonable basis for political decision-making. No republic can flourish without a system of communication that rewards honesty without demanding perfection and attaches costs to insincerity without succumbing to spite.

Nothing that threatens public ownership of the state, and therefore public liberty, can be left safe in private hands. The credit-creating powers of banks and the opinion forming powers of the systems of communication will tend over time to alienate us from effective control of our own lives. More and more of the money we make will be taken from us in the form of interest or monopoly charges for heat, light, food and fresh water. More and more of the beliefs we hold will be shaped by the designs of others and will tend to distract us from the central concern of free citizens, the understanding and control of the shared conditions of life. The integrated systems of knowledge, production and credit, at once gigantic and intricate, could provide us with the means to live and flourish. They will only do so when they are made subject to a sovereign people.

Chapter 4

Maximum Republic

It is necessary for anyone who organizes a republic and establishes laws in it to take for granted that all men are evil and that they will always act according to the wickedness of their nature whenever they have the opportunity.
Machiavelli

In a republic a defined group of citizens owns the state. In a maximally republican constitution, the entire adult population constitutes this state-owning public. The form of the state – the organization of each element, and of the relationships between them – falls within general comprehension and under general control. When the population-as-public acts in ways that it has determined to be lawful it can change the personnel of the state and remake its institutions. Each citizen has an equal claim to ownership of a state that is a collective achievement.

An unwritten or uncodified constitution is not compatible with republican democracy. Customary use is not the same as lawful possession. It follows that it is necessary to codify the rules governing the state. But this codification does not have to limit itself to the ordinary categories of constitutional thought. Given the deep strangeness of our current arrangements we are in a position to see what other countries have achieved and rectify some of their shortcomings. It is not credible to argue for constitutional reform that does not address these shortcomings.

Existing constitutions do not protect nominally sovereign publics from the depredations and deceptions of powerful factions in the state and their allies in the directorate of corporate officers, financiers and controllers of capital. The forms of a democratic republic are all too easy subverted. As Engels noted in 1891, those who make politics their business pose a particular threat:

> *Nowhere do "politicians" form a more separate, powerful section of the nation than in North America. There, each of the two great parties which alternately succeed each other in power is itself in turn controlled by people who make a business of politics, who speculate on seats in the legislative assemblies of the Union as well as of the separate states, or who make a living by carrying on agitation for their party and on its victory are rewarded with positions.*

> *It is well known that the Americans have been striving for 30 years to shake off this yoke, which has become intolerable, and that in spite of all they can do they continue to sink ever deeper in this swamp of corruption. It is precisely in America that we see best how there takes place this process of the state power making itself independent in relation to society, whose mere instrument it was originally intended to be. Here there exists no dynasty, no nobility, no standing army, beyond the few men keeping watch on the Indians, no bureaucracy with permanent posts or the right to pensions. And nevertheless we find here two great gangs of political speculators, who alternately take possession of the state power and exploit it by the most corrupt means and for the most corrupt ends – and the nation is powerless against these two great cartels of politicians, who are ostensibly its servants, but in reality exploit and plunder it.*

To repeat, the aim is not to make the countries in Britain like somewhere else. It is to make them more like themselves. Only by frustrating the ambitions of political speculators will this be possible.

A new constitutional settlement must extend beyond the legislature, executive and judiciary to include the systems of communication. In order to exercise effective ownership of the state, a sovereign public must understand what it possesses. We do not fully own what we do not fully understand. So we need independent powers to investigate the shared world, to discover the preferences of others, and to debate the objectives of political action. It is foolish to hope to remain free without this combination of knowledge and power. The ambitious will always be tempted to advance their interests through fraud. Having misled us they will then declare us incapable of government. They will noisily regret the need to keep certain matters to themselves and say how keenly they look forward to the day when we have evolved sufficiently to take responsibility for ourselves. Until then, though, they will insist that they have no option but to do as they please and use their considerable talents to reconcile us to the consequences.

Public liberty denies this fraud the prestige of the state by placing the same share of sovereign power in every citizen's hands. The state itself becomes a site of participation between equals and the close-up tyrannies of the workplace and of the private sphere can no longer rely on the winking connivance of a central power whose illegitimacy reflects and encourages them. There is no more happy collusion between politicians and financiers. Instead the state becomes their unrushed and remorseless enemy. All of our arrangements, including relations of state and private power, become matters for general review.

Information that supplies the needs of the sovereign public in a large republic can only come from a system of communication that we substantially control. Each citizen needs an equal power to direct investigation and research into the content of the shared world. Each of us needs a further, equal, power to determine what becomes widely known. This is the substance of public commissioning, the basis for a system of communications that works with, and improves, other democratic institutions.[1]

Without such a system most of us are reduced to the status of Bagehot's 'vacant many'. It is very difficult to acquire the information we need to act as public beings. Even if we succeed, most of our fellow citizens will struggle to understand what we are saying, and will have few incentives to try. We turn to the media for entertainment and our appetite for the trivial and the sensational becomes evidence of our civic incompetence. Meanwhile supposedly serious coverage is a kind of fully clothed farce, at once formulaic and fantastical.

Consider what it means to make a plan for one's life in such circumstances. Success for most depends on their joining some set-up that resembles a racket more than a legitimate business. It is possible to do good work, of course, and many people do. But they also become aware that this good work often has little bearing on their chances of promotion or advancement. Sometimes the desire to do right by clients, patients and the public can be career-ending. For the most part if status is what you want it makes more sense to concentrate on work that is socially useless, environmentally dangerous and intellectually indefensible. This breakdown in the relationship between virtue and reward opens the way to a distinctively republican style of critique. For status in a republican system fully achieved rests ultimately on service to the common good, rather than on dutiful service to a privileged minority.

The communications system in Britain, as in any large and sophisticated state, is thoroughly integrated with the rest of the political and economic settlement. But in its current form it cannot host a discussion between equals about its merits and weaknesses. Citizens cannot reliably encounter one another as citizens. The inability of the communications system to describe itself and the wider structure to which it belongs, and its refusal to publicise such descriptions from elsewhere, play an important role in sustaining our arrangements. In normal times this settlement establishes a zone of controversy. What it excludes exists only as kind of private, barely communicable disquiet. We cannot discover the opinions of others, or work effectively to improve the quality of our beliefs or theirs.

A minority control the limits of debate. In a fully achieved republic this control is generalised on egalitarian terms. The effectual public is enlarged to include everyone. We each begin with an equal power to shape the sum of the things that are widely known. Individual deliberation and public debate cause some matters to become more or less prominent. Over time we come to favour some explanations over others. But as individuals we always retain the means to collaborate with others to raise old and new concerns, to expand the range of discussion, to contest the limits of state action, redraw the boundaries of the political, to describe, promote and enact the changes we choose.

We could begin to establish a republican system of communication by making the public subsidies for journalism and research, which are currently as lavish as they are unremarked, subject to public direction. Once pooled these funds would be given to journalists and researchers who persuade some fraction of the public to support them. Large sums will require significant support, small sums will need less. Projects funded by the public will be published in such a way as to reach beyond its commissioning public. Everyone will then have an opportunity to indicate whether they wanted a particular story to be given further publicity. Investigations into matters of widespread or persistent concern would be broadcast, and could perhaps develop into regular features (*Police and Security State Watch*, or *Bank of England News*, say). This isn't about electing representatives and hoping that they will do the right thing. The audience becomes an active commissioning body and the exercise of that function becomes part of what each of us learns about ourselves, and each other. For while it is commonplace to say that education empowers it is also true that power educates.

Some of what the public supports and promotes in this system will be trivial or misconceived. Some of it will be pernicious. But it will also be subject to effective public challenge and refutation.

More than that, everything that is described as a fact of nature, or as too complex for popular understanding, can be made subject to permanent critical review. We will be able to understand and, if we wish, to alter much that is currently held incomprehensible and inevitable. Public sovereignty depends on this power of review, and discovers itself through it.

Most importantly, this approach establishes a thorough separation of the representative institutions of government on the one hand – the Westminster Parliament, the devolved assemblies, councils – and the institutions charged with describing their actions, holding them to account, and outlining the ways in which they might be reformed.

At present the BBC is the buckle that connects the field of general descriptions to the political elite. The BBC is a creature of Parliament and takes it cue from the minority of elected politicians there who control, or plausibly compete for control of, the executive. The private media groups also operate in an environment shaped by political power.[2] They depend on politicians for privileged access, a flow of routine news and front-page scoops and they enjoy significant public subsidies. Exposed as they are to market forces, they have another set of pressures to contend with; they have to create platforms that advertisers are happy to use. In normal times elected politicians and the managers of a centralised and politicised economy find it easy to define politics and the limits of politics. Democracy is representation, not participation, in their thoroughly publicised account.

Freedom as the absence of obvious constraint is widely discussed. Freedom as the power to oversee and direct the state does not feature in the main avenues of intelligence and information. Given that we are kept under close surveillance and the public sphere is subject to all kinds of manipulation this pattern of speech and silence is perhaps to be expected. Most of us can go about our business without feeling too obviously hemmed in. But others have shaped the environment in which we make our decisions. Others have produced the information on which we make our decisions. This is unfreedom at its most refined. Advancement depends on a very delicate attitude towards the facts of our conditions. Somehow we must both know and not know the limits of what is permitted.

Individual politicians are vulnerable to the media and individual journalists are vulnerable to politicians. But the media are structurally vulnerable to the politicians and politics is structurally vulnerable to the media. Consider for a moment what happened to Rupert Murdoch's attempt to take full control of Sky when Parliament decided to stop him. Consider, too, what would have happened if the *News of the World*'s archive of unpublished photographs and documents had seen the light of day. And yet, as Tony Blair pointed out a few years ago, 'the problem for the public is that they are totally reliant on what the media give them for their view of politics'. Given this cat's cradle of dependencies only a fool would expect a reliable account of power to become widely available, without wide-ranging reform of the communications sector.[3]

Liberal constitution builders in the eighteenth century sought to divide the executive, legislative and judicial powers of the state and to establish a tension between democratic, aristocratic and monarchical elements. Their concern was to prevent a concentration of power capable of overwhelming all opposition. But first the commercial newspapers and then the radio, film and television industries gave insiders new powers to shape public opinion. The parties and their allies in the private economy were able to monopolize state power, since the formal separation of powers co-existed with an effectual fusion of the media and the political system.

Since we depend on intermediate institutions to discover what elected officials are doing, we must exercise a degree of direct power over these institutions if we want to remain tolerably well informed. The power to govern and the power to describe government cannot rest in the same hands. That much is obvious. But neither can we leave the job of holding the state and private interests to account to a few media executives who benefit hugely from the current arrangements, and who are exquisitely vulnerable to pressure from those they are required to invigilate. The explicit separation of legislative, executive and judicial power on the one hand from the power to describe them on the other is necessary if we wish to live in substantively democratic societies. The natural repository of control over this power to describe is the people who are the voting, viewing and tweeting public. In this way we check the power of elected representatives and corporate employees through direct public control of resources, rather than through yet more elected representatives. At present elections take place against a background of inadequate general understanding. We cannot expect the communications system to improve if we leave the task to those who can currently win, or plausibly hope to win, elections.

Reform along these lines does not depend on the abolition of the monarchy, changes to the voting system, or any other narrowly 'constitutional' change. There is nothing to prevent us from working to secure it now, in the existing order. The spreading recognition that popular sovereignty depends on a public organization of knowledge is itself progress towards the achievement of that sovereignty. Every success in making the publicly funded and subsidised media subject to meaningful public oversight and control makes the country more fully republican now, through adjustments in existing institutions, and through advances in individual understanding.

A republican system of communication will not stop at journalism. It is bound to extend over the whole field of knowledge. It will come to include the discussion and then the conduct of science. The state, the corporations and a handful of industrial and post-industrial foundations largely determine the distribution of scientific curiosity. This distribution has important implications for the rest of society. One prominent figure in science policy in America in the 1960s reckoned that the 2% of GDP the state then spent on research and development had 'disproportionate social and economic leverage, since the whole thrust of the economy is determined by scientific and technical research.'[4] Though there is some scope for independent, and occasionally even disruptive, research, the bulk of the money goes to those who refine their curiosity until it is consistent with the needs and interests of those who control the funds. As Harold Laski noted as far back as 1928, 'it is merely the fact that a fund is in reach that permeates everything. The college develops along the lines the foundation approves. The dependence is merely implicit, but is in fact quite final'.[5]

Although science reflects the preoccupations and assumptions of those who fund it, scientists do not always like to admit this elementary fact. So the existing organization of science remains obscure. Much useful work is still done but private acquisitiveness and *raison d'état* determine most of the ends to which scientific methods are applied. A science that is open to direction by a freely associating public will create news kinds of knowledge and new ways of winning renown. The disinterested desire to help others will have a more secure place in the necessarily mixed motives that drive research. Given the pressing need to reorganize industrial production in order to prevent catastrophic climate change, and the failure of the current system to allocate the necessary resources, a republican science becomes all the more attractive. Very cheap energy that does not damage the environment would be a great achievement. But it would spell disaster for some of the most powerful private interests on the planet. Absent the public, concern for the public interest in science is only a kind of wistfulness.

The acquisition by the public of powers to direct inquiry will steadily transform the content and purposes of the communications system. The news agenda will no longer be presented as the reflection of an objective reality. It will be debated widely and its priorities will reflect the expressed wishes of individual citizens and the associations they form. The public's power to direct inquiry will range across disciplinary boundaries. We will be able to contemplate without blinking the irreducibly political dimensions of both social and natural science. The swindle of invented complexity will be more difficult to sustain, as will the various ruses that substitute sentiment for understanding. Journalists will not decide what is, and isn't, newsworthy in perfect seclusion from the public gaze.

None of this is inconsistent with the existence of free private media, or with the public service ethos in broadcasting. A republican system of knowledge must welcome the test of alternative descriptions, and invite challenge and correction, since it can only call itself republican if it does so. But nothing can be considered beyond the reach of such a system. All claims that cannot survive general scrutiny will be rejected, including those, especially those, relating to power and knowledge and the relationship between them.

The notion that the public should have a degree of control over the public sphere, and some say in determining its content, strikes many people as absurd or sinister. They discern in current patterns of media consumption an eternal truth about the incompetence of the majority to govern itself. Opponents of public liberty often think of themselves as liberals and progressives. Perhaps they are, but they are also the enemies of republican democracy. Without the power to direct inquiry we are helpless to do more than applaud options set before us in a process we do not understand. The majority become a prop for elite self-confidence, conferring mandates that can be further interpreted according to elite needs. The public in such circumstances does not understand, it is understood, it does not interpret, it is interpreted. It performs much the same function as a disembowelled beast in a ritual of augury.

Republican ownership of the state cannot be made subject to an external limit. No power that affects the whole can be left unexamined in private hands. The public of a republic determines the extent, and limits, of state action. It is the only arbiter of the political and as such has a right to intervene in the communications system as it chooses. General participation in this is a precondition for the establishment of a maximum republic. But this will only be possible when we have put aside our fear and hatred of each other.

Most of us are vulnerable to arbitrary power to a greater or lesser extent. At work we are tempted to become flatterers, and to deceive ourselves in order to work the necessary deceits on others. We are what we are because of the circumstances in which we find ourselves, and the incentives those circumstances generate. In Britain our captivity is so thoroughly achieved that it can become a kind of cosiness. To imagine the end of Radio 4 is to imagine the end of the world.[6] As we change our circumstances we will change ourselves, and become better suited to the demands of liberty, better able to appreciate the pleasures of candour.

Of course, there is a danger implicit in this. The enemies of republican rule point out that we can tear down the checks on power for which we alone are responsible. We cannot rely on any authority to protect us from our own power or to preserve that power on our behalf. Our enemies are right. Everything that is necessary for government and self-government, including the power to commission widely shared descriptions of the world, belongs to us only for as long as we remain mindful and undaunted. An unrelenting effort of suspicion is needed to prevent some fraction from subjugating the whole, to prevent us from willing our own subjugation. But we cannot live in freedom without this threat. The possibility of despotism is a necessary condition for public liberty. If a state is safe from falling into despotism, it is only because it is already despotic.

Once we establish control over the subsidies that support the structures of knowledge and sentiment we can at last begin to discuss the world in an orderly and reasoned way. This discussion will not depend on the luridly coloured stories of the popular media, or the respectful stenography of the serious press. We will no longer have to surrender to the queasy dynamics of sensational entertainment or the demands of power worship.

This doesn't mean that we will suddenly gain reliable access to an unchanging objective reality. The world beyond our direct experience will continue to be mediated by others. But we will be able to subject the accounts we are offered to a continuous test. We will discuss as equals what we know and what we need to know. We will do so confident that we can all effectively challenge unsupported assertions, shaky logic and outright fabrications. We will all have the means to act in ways that have a public character, that make a difference to the shared world.

A system of communications organized on these lines will be open to all points of view. Nothing that is currently suppressed or marginalised and that has advocates will lack opportunities for audible and visible expression. It is almost impossible to conceive of this reconciliation of publicity and the public world, so ingrained are we in patterns that assign passive silence to the majority and noisy authority to the few. Those who control widely publicised speech will complain that the majority cannot be trusted with work that requires their very special qualities of mind. They keep the airwaves free of trash. They draw the line and maintain certain standards of decency. These the mob will sweep away. But though there is some truth in what they say, the tidiness cannot compensate us for the loss of what is tidied away. If we are capable of citizenship, then we are capable of reason, even if it will take us some time to bring our beliefs into line with the best available information. For a while there will be a riot of wild claims and lurid assertions. Some of them will be true.

Besides, claims that do not bear serious examination already routinely pass unchallenged in the circuits of widely publicised speech. The economy is described in colourful language that leaves audiences doubting the evidence afforded them by direct experience. War becomes a humanitarian obligation rather than an instrument of policy. Politicians pretend that politics is what elected politicians say and do. Hence the exercise of power by those who aren't elected is discussed as if it is outside politics or ignored altogether. Britain's particular brand of capitalism is treated as an inevitable and incorrigible fact of nature. The possibility of another capitalism, let alone a democratic alternative to capitalism, scarcely features. The media concur in all this and attempts to challenge this lock on political speech are characterised as spasms of moral outrage.　　　　　•

Our inability to challenge the claims of the powerful creates endless traps for the unwary. This problem is perhaps most glaring in the related matters of money – a constant preoccupation for most of us – and monetary policy – a thing of deep and forbidding mystery. Adam Smith once remarked that 'all money is matter of belief'. The question is this, what kind of belief befits a free people? Blind faith, or reasoned understanding?

In ordinary times the guardians of the currency promote what they themselves call superstitions in order to maintain 'discipline in the allocation of resources' and to prevent 'chaos and inefficiency'.[7] Needless to say, the chaotic inefficiency of the system protected by these superstitions does not worry them much. One of these myths is the idea that monetary policy can ever be anything other than a political matter. Consider this remark from the resignation speech of a Conservative Chancellor, Norman Lamont, in 1993:

I do not believe that even the timing of interest rate changes should ever be affected by political considerations. Interest rate changes should never be used to offset some unfavourable political event …

The time has come to make the Bank of England independent.[8]

According to Geoffrey Robinson, a few years later in 1997 the future Labour Chancellor Gordon Brown was 'struck by how American interest-rate movements were not a political issue'. In a meeting with Brown, Alan Greenspan, the head of the Federal Reserve, told Brown that it was '"unfair" to expect politicians to take unpopular decisions on interest rates'.[9] The scene Robinson describes, of a politician being won over to the merits of independent central banking, has been taking place all over the Western world for a generation. But the alternative to control of the interest rate by elected politicians is not, and cannot be apolitical. It is undemocratic, but it is still political.

In March 2007 the former governor of the Bank of England, Eddie George, told the Treasury Select Committee that the bank had cut interest rates in the early years of the century in order to prevent a recession. He acknowledged that the bank's actions had 'pushed' consumer spending to 'levels which couldn't possibly be sustained into the medium and long term'. George explained that this 'pushed up house prices, it increased household debt ... my legacy to the MPC if you like has been "sort that out"'.[10] Months later Northern Rock collapsed and it became clear that the increase of private sector debt encouraged by the central bank posed a serious threat to the national economy.

The decision to raise or lower the cost of money has far-reaching distributional effects. Very high interest rates in the late seventies and early eighties were part of a concerted effort in both Britain and the United States to transfer wealth and power from labour to capital. At the time the talk was of the overriding need to fight inflation. Though this convinced some sophisticated audiences, recent history has made a mockery of that explanation. When the global economy looked set to collapse under the weight of more than a decade of reckless credit expansion, central banks around the world began cutting interest rates rapidly. The Bank of England brought them down from 5% in September 2008 to 0.5% in March 2009. They have remained there ever since, even though inflation has been above the target rate for most of this period.[11] The stated aim of the policy, to support lending to the wider economy, has not been achieved. But low interest rates have given private banks time to repair their balance sheets while avoiding significant reforms.

The banking system was put on life support after its high-speed collision with economic reality. The decision to save it can only ever be understood if we see it for what it was, a supremely political decision. The central banks saved the private banks because they share the same, essentially political, vision of how society should be organized. The financial sector as the creators of new money determined how effective demand is distributed in the economy. They remain central because the managers of the state cannot imagine an alternative. Emergency measures like quantitative easing have far-reaching economic effects and should also be called what they are – political interventions to support some interests at the expense of others.

Because banks determine how demand is distributed in the economy, they determine how the economy develops and who gets what. This is an extraordinary power.[12] As such it should be brought into the light of the constitutional settlement. When the crisis struck, central bankers could not bring themselves to imagine a world where they didn't run the economy in partnership with private banks. Central bankers provided the wisdom and the perspective and private bankers provided the animal spirits. It was the perfect amalgam of reason and desire. The mere fact of disastrous failure could not be permitted to disrupt something so beautiful, so gratifying to everyone who understood it.

Putting an end to all this will not be possible until it is widely understood. But once thoroughly investigated and discussed it can be changed. Even now we can see some of the first steps towards effective reform. Let's start with something uncontroversial from a renowned authority on economics and pillar of the establishment. Martin Wolf is the associate editor of the *Financial Times* and a former member of the UK government's Independent Commission on Banking. In a book published before the financial crisis he argued that 'the management of any systematically important bank that has to be rescued by the state should be disbarred, as a matter of course, from further work in the financial industry'. He went on to say:

> *Remember the fundamental point. Big banks have consistently operated in the knowledge that their profits are private and losses, if large enough, public. In other words, the institutions they run are underpinned by the state. Managers are, in an important sense, public servants. If they abuse that trust, they should be treated accordingly.*[13]

Wolf was quite right about this, although he hasn't repeated the point since crisis engulfed British and American, as opposed to Asian, banks. It follows that we must now relieve the entire management of the financial sector of their onerous responsibilities for creating credit and directing investment. They obviously can't help but act recklessly and we are being, to borrow a word from Alan Greenspan, unfair if we expect them to change. The condominium of central bankers and the financial sector has failed.

Bankers can't be left to create money in a cloud of mystical-technocratic squid ink. Like the circuits of publicity, the circuits of credit must be made subject to effective public oversight and substantial public control. Money will always have a meaning. What money means now – government by the financial sector and by holders of capital – cannot be stated out loud. It is a secret whispered among the elect. But the only sure guardians of the public faith and credit are the public. If we are ultimately on the hook for the money that's created by banks, then we need to make sure it is lent into existence in the service of ends to which we give our reasoned support, for which we are willing to work. In a maximally republican system credit comes under democratic control. In such a settlement credit can be used to restructure the economy so that no one is subject to powers they cannot challenge. Furthermore, public control of credit breaks the monopoly power of private capital. If private investors will not invest, the public can.

A publicly controlled credit system will naturally favour those institutional forms that best serve the wider public interest. Over time we can expect an expanded role for the cooperative and employee-owned sector and preferential treatment for companies that adopt a simple and candid approach in their dealings with the tax authorities. Lending money to private equity groups that aggressively avoid tax is less attractive than lending money to employee-controlled trusts that share incomes more equally and are more closely tied to the fortunes of the places where they operate.

A public that directs both the production of knowledge and the creation of new money has the means to govern its own affairs. But as Stuart White has noted a republican economy that only gave each citizen an equal voice in private investment decisions would fall short of what is needed.[14] After all, a continually expanding consumer economy threatens to destroy industrial civilization. On the other hand, the investments in public goods necessary to avert environmental disaster or improve human welfare will often tend to reduce the size of the market economy. Steps necessary to avert environmental collapse might improve our quality of life while reducing the sum of monetary exchanges.

Substantial public funds are already available for research into the provision of these necessary public goods, more than enough to shape the direction of the economy as a whole. Secretive and unaccountable control of these funds has been tried and has been found wanting. General participation in decisions about the use of these subsidies will provide what economists claim the market gives us – the best possible information about what people actually want. But it also gives many of us the prospect of rewarding work and opportunities for useful heroism.

In most of us the desire for the general good is weak and intermittent, while concern for our own welfare, and for the welfare of those we love, is steady and strong. This has caused some to despair of popular government. But a body politic made up of largely self-regarding individuals need not be anything like as short-sighted and ungenerous as the individuals who constitute it. While self-interest is strong, it constantly expends itself in conflict with the self-interest of others. At best it resolves into competing and unstable factions. On the other hand, while disinterested concern for the common good is weak, it gains strength from the disinterest it finds elsewhere. In the words of Katrin Oddsdóttir, one of the members of the Icelandic Constitutional Assembly, 'there is a brilliance in the crowd that is greater than the sum of the individuals in it'.[15]

We can't predict in detail how a sovereign public will divide its efforts between general improvement and the pursuit of individual advantage. But we can take a degree of comfort from the fact that the public is better able to discover and achieve the public interest than any one of its constituent members. To put it another way, republican control of public funds for scientific and technological research give us the best possible means to align private ambition with the common good.

Public control of credit and investment will not come until we collectively control the field of generally shared descriptions. This in turn will eventually require changes to the constitution. But, to repeat, we do not have to wait to begin reorganizing the economy on republican lines. The decision to act as if one had a public status is the bulk of what it means to be a citizen. The individual who works with others to secure public liberty is already visiting the republic she hopes to settle permanently.

Chapter 5

From Here to There

The English people believes itself to be free: it is gravely mistaken; it is free only during election of members of parliament; as soon as the members are elected, the people are enslaved; it is nothing. In the brief moment of its freedom, the English people make such a use of that freedom that it deserves to lose it.
Jean-Jacques Rousseau

There are as many ideal constitutions as there are idealists. But the principle is clear. A democratic republic worthy of the name is one in which we all hold an equal share in the institutions that together comprise the state. In the past reformers put their faith in representation through the ballot box. Paine was typical in expecting that universal suffrage and regular elections would prevent governments from waging aggressive war as a pretext for increasing taxes. Elected officials would be restrained by the electorate and forced to serve their interests.

History has shown that national governments – especially in large, steeply unequal countries – are able to invent all manner of fictions in order to exalt themselves and keep 'the vast mass of mankind in the background of the human picture'.[1] War is only one pretext among many. Meanwhile, stable party systems keep political office in the hands of those who understand that their public eminence depends on private submission to those who control the avenues of publicity and advancement.

Nominally constitutional governments manipulate the systems of education and communication to ensure that they remain at least one step away from effective control by the citizen body. Through a chain of pretended necessities they favour certain sectors through more or less covert subsidies, through changes to legislation and through control of the permanent administration. The centralised economy delivers both super profits and a workforce that is caught up in a system of arbitrary penalties and rewards that would once have been called tyrannical. The modern workplace is a playground for the insincere, a nightmare for the candid.

The private economy becomes a client of the state. The wealthy and their counterparts in government form an alliance based on mutual self-interest and the awareness that both political and economic inequality depend on popular confusion. This partnership has always made politics a lucrative business. Enlarge businesses through government patronage and they can easily afford to employ former politicians as lobbyists, advisers and board members. But, remember, the payments have something of the quality of a protection racket, since the fortunes amassed by bankers and others are intensely vulnerable to state action. The cartels of politicians described in Engels are still very much in business. And in Britain the fortunes to be made in politics are greater than ever.

The Americans have created a criminal-imperial system under the cover of constitutional government. Both the War on Drugs and the War on Terror provide pretexts for monitoring, manipulating and defrauding a nominally sovereign people. The military and intelligence institutions also allow a few well-placed individuals and families to extort money from wealthy foreigners. But more broadly, those on the inside can make the political system a device for frustrating the public good. They do so above all by shaping the systems of communication on which the public rely on for information about the world beyond their immediate experience. Plainly, regular elections on the basis of universal suffrage are not enough.

In Britain the absence of a constitution exacerbates the menace posed by the state. When they think they are speaking out of earshot our spies boast about the country's 'more permissive legal environment'.[2] Meanwhile, the British media system ensures that both the government and the opposition have extensive opportunities to reach a national audience. A handful of people set the tenor for coverage across the field of publicity. To a very large extent politics is what the party leaderships say it is. In theory individual members of Parliament could take an independent line, but the close integration of the executive and the legislature has encouraged the ambitious to do what they are told and blame the supernatural powers of the Whips' office for their obedience since, in Burke's words, 'like Janissaries they derive a kind of freedom from the very condition of their servitude'.[3] This exaltation through humiliation weaves through the magico-libidinal fabric of the traditional constitution.

There are signs that the hold over individuals by the party system is beginning to weaken slightly. Some of the more bloody-minded MPs are using new technology to build relationships with the public that do not depend on party preferment or on patronage from the print and broadcast media. But most are still too stupid or avid for office to do much more than parrot their front bench on Twitter. Reform will come from outside Parliament, or it will not come at all.

This is not to say that we can free ourselves in isolation. Rejecting Parliament's monopoly on political speech does not mean withdrawing from the electoral process. Our liberation, after all, depends on the liberation of others. Certainly we need to inquire for ourselves, and to reflect on what we learn. But if we are serious about liberty, we also need new opportunities to talk with one another as equals. What is required is a parallel system of communication and decision-making, an embryonic republic that first regulates and then reforms the Parliamentary system on lines that are widely debated and that secure general assent.

This, then, is the first step towards a fully republican constitution; the creation by citizens of assemblies – in the material world, as much as online – where individuals meet one another and constitute themselves as publics with defined purposes and rules of conduct. These publics will orientate themselves towards specific ends within the wider project of securing effective popular sovereignty. Absent assembly, there is no body politic, no public that can animate and direct a democratic state.

Assemblies, in the sense of structured opportunities for people to both speak and listen, are profoundly at odds with representation. In a parliamentary system politicians present themselves to the public in terms that they think will be appealing. They impersonate the national mood, in order to both give it substantial form and to make it amenable to their leadership. The forms of speech in this representative system are, to repeat, manipulative to their marrow. Politicians pose as figures of unreal certainty, all the while striving to appear ordinary. The public is an object to be worked on and swayed by synthetic personalities using themes informed and refined by detailed market research. In an assembly, people listen and speak and revise their views through conversation and further study elsewhere. The decisions made are important in themselves and they provide valuable information about the preferences of others. But the process of individual and collective transformation is central. The parliamentary system is a broadcast state. Republican democracy, fully realised, is a conversational state.

At the moment regular panel discussions and occasional candidates' debates offer a version of politics in which most of us are expected to watch and listen in silence. Perhaps if we are lucky we will get to ask a question. But the privilege of answering is given to the figures on the stage. The show confirms the difference between those who decide and those who must live with the decisions. Our role is to choose the political leader we like, the one that seems to speak to us - the one whose communications team has been most adroit in its handling of the temper of the people. In an assembly, on the other hand, while professional politicians can, of course, speak, the game is not rigged in their favour. They are open to challenge in ways that are not permitted in the parliamentary model.

A change comes over us, when we can speak to others as equals. We are able to reason without regard for institutional position or private status. We can begin to consider matters that are normally ignored or misrepresented. Much of the sadness that afflicts us as individuals has its origins in our collective arrangements, in the structure of incentives and threats with which we live, in the descriptions of human flourishing that the communications industry promote. The remedy is not to be found in drugs or therapy but in political, social and economic change. If we are responsible for our lives, we must have the power to change the circumstances in which we live. Responsibility without power is the predicament of the depressive. On the other hand, our happiness depends, at least in part, on our conversing as equals. Liberty, in the sense of shared ownership of a conversational state, is good for us.

Our new power seems to be inside us. We experience a kind of exhilaration when we become conscious of our freedom. This exhilaration is visible to others. But this freedom-as-power is not our individual achievement or possession. It is a common property that depends on our being recognised by others as someone with a right to speak effectually, to be heard and to be reckoned with. This is the world-changing power. It is brought into being by our conferring public status on others through respectful attention, candid debate and attention to the common good.[4]

The settled world luxuriates in misunderstanding this. It exalts the timid conformist and declares the machine politician and assiduous climber of hierarchies a maverick free thinker. A captive media tell us that men of vision rule us, that their eminence derives from their excellence. The politicians themselves become enthralled by self-pity. Clinton watched *High*

Noon repeatedly in the White House, joining a long line of Presidents whose careers were built on craven service to outlaws, yet saw themselves as the lonely defenders of an ungrateful township. The lie repeats itself endlessly, that trust and representation have already given us what we can only secure through suspicion and participation.

As we assemble in conditions of equality we experience the truth, that we each have some role in creating liberty as power. Power is no longer a frustrating will-o-the-wisp, always just out of reach. It derives from those that are subject to it, as always, but now it is their common possession. This discovery brings great benefits. Thoughts that have no place in the circuits of ordinarily audible speech cease to cause us distress. Individuals speak with some expectation of being heard. Subjects deemed inadmissible, disreputable or irrelevant are held up to the daylight of general inquiry. The self-pitying guardians of inequality no longer set the limits of what can be said. If we are wrong, we are met with argument rather than ridicule.

Instead of the dynamics of a broadcast, where a few speak and the vast majority sit in attentive silence, assemblies come closer to the ideal of public speech, where as many people speak as listen. No one decides in advance what the assembly can and cannot discuss. The resulting deliberation and debate exposes the necessary fictions of the existing order to a new, shared understanding.

The process is frustrating. It has none of the easy appeal of the spectacular politics we are used to. Most people have not dedicated themselves to the art of seeming pleasant and sympathetic. In fact our fellow citizens are often annoying. More than that, something is at stake. If we matter, then our errors matter. Everyone has their own, ideal, outcome in mind and everyone is bound to be disappointed. But better this than the flattery of the election campaign, where the candidate gestures towards what the majority of voters want before he or she disavows those gestures in office. Did your favourite seem to promise that they would do what you wanted? You must have been mistaken. Never mind, another professional of speech will come along in four years time and seem to promise to make it up to you.

In a democracy of equals we give up the fantasy that someone else can give us our heart's desire. In exchange we take what we need if we are to flourish as free adults – a share in the permanently unfinished and unsatisfactory project of governing ourselves. Our liberation is a disaster for those who seek power, since it deprives them of what they most crave, the chance to embody 'the temper of the people' and so become, at least for a while, larger than life. All candidates, always, seek the condition of divinity, whether they admit it or not. This does not necessarily mean that we should do without elected officials. But the gains to be had from full-time politicians must be weighted against the dangers they pose to everyone else. All too often they exalt themselves by debasing the rest of us. Great care needs to be taken if we are to ensure that their individual prestige is tied securely to promotion of the common good.

Recent history gives us some sense of the difference assembly can make. The use of public spaces in Madrid and hundreds of other cities in 2011 created a public power. Occupation was a shared risk that led those involved to believe that they were somehow consequential. These were people who lived in formal democracies – Spain, the United States, Great Britain, and elsewhere. They had grown up hearing that to assemble as sovereign citizens was unnecessary, or impossible. But they gathered anyway, and began to experience what it feels like to be free. Politics ceased to be something that one watched from a distance and became something that one did. The decision to act created a shared freedom to shape events. The assembly provided a medium in which this freedom could be exercised. The occupiers determined what happened in each place, they were responsible for what was said in their name. By acting as though they mattered, they discovered what had always been true – that the assembly of people is the beginning of power.

Thousands of people experienced something of how it feels to be given and give power, because each occupation adopted a very similar structure for deliberation and decision. Much time has been spent clucking about the shortcomings of the assembly principle. The critics of the occupations liked to complain about the lack of shared principles and demands. They rarely notice this awesome unanimity of method. It is almost as though they are worried that others might be curious to sample public speech – and the power it implies – for themselves. The method is what matters. And sure enough, it is the method that vanishes in the accounts of enemies and false friends.

Assemblies do not operate on the basis of simple majority rule. Individuals who disagree can block or at least delay proposals and statements of principle they do not support. Proceedings do not degenerate into a scramble to secure enough votes to overcome opposition. There is instead a bias towards a full exploration of contending points of view. The opportunity to speak with some expectation of being heard is no longer the preserve of a few. Of course this makes them exquisitely vulnerable to manipulation and disruption. As such they are contemptible to those who worship power.

Nevertheless, each time we assemble as equals we have a chance to escape the exhausted and exhausting common sense on freedom that has muddled so many of us for so long. We can experience what Abraham Lincoln described, the inseparable link between government and self-government. We can appreciate that being free is about more than being left alone, indeed that freedom requires the opposite of solitude, encounter with others whose autonomy cannot be ignored. Freedom in this sense includes control over one's immediate environment. Fully realised it encompasses the power to shape the state, even the power to fold it up and put it away.

Most people have few opportunities to experience equality in speech. If we are serious about securing change, then it is up to us to create venues where liberty becomes a matter of lived experience. After all, no programme can be justified if it is not understood and approved by those affected. Whatever we want, however we understand our politics, we need assemblies as a medium for general deliberation between equals. As we establish more assemblies in which people can speak as equals, we can learn about each other, and develop forms of understanding that do not derive from the calculations of editors, producers and party managers. And if we gather in sufficient numbers we will secure the power needed to enact this new knowledge of the world. Each assembly constituted on republican lines becomes a machine for creating public liberty.

The occupations achieved what they achieved through visible and obtrusive transgression. People behaved in ways that were not mandated by, or welcome to, the governing powers. They used space for their own purposes and they asserted their right to decide. In London the occupiers turned their backs on the police who were kettling them in the churchyard of St Paul's and began the first of many assemblies. Faced with the agents of formal authority, citizens looked instead to one another. Deprived of an opposition, the police could no longer define the meaning of the situation. They came expecting a protest and found instead the beginnings of a body politic. For a moment a few thousand citizens were sovereign in the space they chose. This was something far more troubling than a crowd, or even a mob. A crowd can be kettled. A mob can be hit with sticks. But what does it mean to kettle people who have no intention of going anywhere?

The sensation of trespass made people feel that what they were doing mattered, and that change was possible. Trespass quickened the occupiers. It seemed that the current order could be picked apart, and that something new could be made from the pieces. Trespass, then, on the prerogatives of politicians and their friends in the media. Trespass on the field of publicity. To be powerful is to speak with confidence that you will be heard. Begin to speak about sites of decision where your opinion matters little, but where the opinions of a few thousand become decisive: the parliamentary constituencies.

Politicians can only take account of developments that threaten their power, their freedom to speak and to decide. Each assembly that meets in a constituency and gives electors a chance to talk freely among themselves presents just such a threat. For all that the discussion of politics is framed in national terms, British politics operates on a territorial basis. Every candidate must secure the support of the largest single fraction of the voters in a geographically defined constituency.

Assemblies don't have to take a self-consciously radical form. Nor do they have to favour those who are already most confident and therefore most likely to speak. Different groups can assemble on their own terms and engage with other assemblies as they see fit. We only learn how to use power by becoming powerful and we will not establish a republic worthy of the name if we blithely reproduce the currently existing distribution of power.

To the full extent possible assembly in the constituencies needs to be supported by online spaces where voters can learn about each others' voting intentions against a background of information about the constituencies' current political complexion. The technology allows us to communicate without the need for a central organizing intelligence. It also allows us to express our differences and discover common ground in a much more nuanced way than is possible with opinion polling. Each of us can become better informed about 'the temper of the people'. More than that, we can reason with one another – perhaps change each others' minds a little, certainly change our own. The more we communicate candidly, under the sign of the public interest, the more we will trust each other.

The same technology delivers enormous benefits to the intelligence agencies. It enables those guardians of the old order to move among the people and gauge their opinions, the better to govern. But that does not mean that we can or should abandon social media, email or any other technology. The state has sought to infiltrate and control any and all spaces where they fear resistance. The assembly – especially in the form of the town hall meeting – has always been a point of particular interest. But both online and real world assemblies can be reclaimed for republican purposes.

The threat to 'Anglo-Saxon capitalism' that a republican culture poses cannot help but provoke a response. Deliberation in assembly online is every bit as vulnerable to manipulation as its physical world equivalent. There is no point denying that. We should instead learn to route around state infiltration and manipulation. (Certain principles are worth bearing in mind here. If something is too good to be true, it isn't true. Be very wary of anyone who advocates law-breaking. We are almost always wrong first time round.) Candid speech between equals is the basis for a new constitutional settlement. As such the guardians will want to derail it. But there is only so much they can do, if we treat their attempts to encourage mutual distrust as evidence that we are making progress.

The political nation sustained by broadcast can, if we want, be replaced by a confederation of informed publics. To be sure this will require us all to learn new habits of speech. Rather than howling like frustrated outsiders we will have to learn how to be civil and measured if we want to be heard. We will have to learn how to filter out insincere as well as hateful speech. Above all, we will have to learn that the exclusion or denigration of any group or individual offends against our own liberty, since we cannot be secure if others can be harmed without cause. Instead of consoling ourselves with the privileges allowed us, we will instead have to fight for our own liberty by defending others.

The consolations of a political settlement built on division will have to give way to the indivisible liberty of the republic.

By threatening to end the careers of individual politicians locally organized publics can begin to secure change. Most of us can be taken for granted by politicians. We sit alone. Perhaps we are entranced by the brand associations of one or other of a few parties. Perhaps we busy ourselves with our private concerns. Either way we learn the same lesson every day, that we are different from, and hateful to, each other. Once we meet beyond the reach of those who currently shape public speech we can discover the interests we hold in common, and trace the lines that still divide us. We can begin to engage with elected representatives not as complaining customers or as petitioning subjects, but as equals.

To a politician a single voter is a nuisance. But a few hundred or a few thousand voters assembled in one place make them anxious. At first our representatives will respond, with the help of the unreformed media, by imitating and appropriating discontent. They will express our anger, the better to channel it away from the powerful and toward the appropriate scapegoats – immigrants, people on welfare, whatever social sadism seems most likely to secure electoral advantage without disturbing the governing consensus we have instead of a constitution. They will pretend that they say what they say because they are in mystic communion with the country's decent, hard-working families. But in the end these professionals of speech will come, and seek to be heard. You will be amazed by their eagerness to attend meetings they did nothing to organize, indeed, did their best to prevent. Let them speak, by all means, on terms agreeable to the assembly.

The more that we assemble and speak without accepting the limits imposed by the established powers, the more we will threaten the existing order, and the more we will force it to change. As numerous assemblies in one constituency become aware of their preferences, become conscious of their shared interests as well as their differences, they exert ever greater pressure on their elected representative. Politicians have risen by learning the rough calculus of serving those who have the power to harm them. Assemblies that change voting patterns cannot be ignored.

There's no point trying to predict what constituency-based assemblies will do with their new opportunities for knowledge and free action. Some might seek to mobilize support for a party committed to a democratic-republican programme. Other might support one of the existing parties, albeit on the most favourable terms possible. Perhaps citizens will use the assembly form to learn what the candidates have to say about matters that concern them, perhaps that will extract a commitment to support a republican constitution.

In each instance action can be informed by a clear-eyed assessment of the relative strength of the incumbent parliamentary system and the insurgent movement for republicanism. The election is a rare moment when the public can influence events. It would be good to use assembly to maximize that influence, in such a way that on the morning after the votes are counted a movement for republican reform has visibly influenced the outcome.[5]

Before the election Scotland will hold a referendum on independence. Whatever happens in September 2014, the months to come are an opportunity for the Scots, and for others in the British Isles, to discuss the nature of modern constitutional government and to do so in ways that enact a republican reality. Scottish independence is attractive because it would mark the end of the traditional constitution in at least one part of the United Kingdom. But the cause will become irresistible in Scotland and the rest of the United Kingdom if it leads to the creation of a vibrantly democratic public culture, through changes to the systems of communication, credit and the corporate form.

Such a vision for Scotland will not be sit comfortably with elected politicians, who will want only those constitutional innovations that leave their prerogatives intact. Representation they understand and can manage. But a newly independent nation has a chance to do things differently. The referendum debate in Scotland offers the rest of Britain the chance to begin a constitutional convention. Perhaps people in the English regions will recognize in the Scottish independence movement a desire for a democratic revolution that they share. Perhaps they will even be moved to consider what self-government in the twenty-first century looks like.

A republican movement is about more than the great set pieces of the next couple of years, the 2014 referendum and the 2015 election. Some assemblies will prefer to concentrate on developing republican institutions and fostering a culture of democratic candour. Assemblies online and in the real world could become spaces in which plans for economic and social development are developed and funded. They could identify economic opportunities and create mutual and cooperatively owned enterprises to meet them. After all, republicanism without economic equality will soon degenerate into oligarchy. But, to repeat, the assemblies will do what they want.

Once in place these institutions could become sources of funds for larger scale projects to bring the local economy under more substantial democratic control. In time local government could become thoroughly integrated with the assembled citizen body. This citizen body could dispose of funds that derive from its shared ownership of the economy. Spending income from the socially controlled sector would be a matter for the population as a whole, convened as a public. In time, and with the minimum of drama, properly constituted publics could also take the power to spend tax revenues.

Those who insist on the need for a global solution to global problems are right. But action in a constituency or a region is of global significance if it demonstrates that even the British are experimenting with a different kind of politics. People in other nations will take notice of what we do, if it gives them some practical ideas as to how they can bring their national governments under greater democratic control. The prospect of democracy in Britain would terrify oligarchy in America.

The institutions of British civil society offer still further venues for trespass in assembly. We have many mass membership organizations. As members most of us receive little more than the occasional email and, very occasionally, a chance to vote for a new leader. Information and power are drawn up to, and hoarded at, the centre. The members are, from the point of view of their administrators, elected or not, a problem to be solved, innocents that must be kept ignorant of disturbing complexities, offered instead the reassuring clarity of the official position on this or that issue.

This is not a criticism of those who run these institutions. Only a few of them are downright cynical or corrupt. Most feel that they manage others for their own good. But if they are ambitious and talented enough to reach the top of their organizations, they cannot be expected to hand their power to shape events to those below them. They have skills and knowledge others lack, they tell themselves. They have no option but to rule. Unaccountable power persists because it is enormous fun for those who wield it, even if, especially if, they are convinced of their democratic good faith.

Imagine the trade unions, the human rights and environmental organizations, the large charities, and the churches, enlivened by the principle of assembly. A vast, but largely dormant, strength resides in these organizations. It is deliberation between equals that will put that strength to work at social transformation. At the moment their members have their gaze fixed upwards, towards those who monopolise decisions. If they look around they will find people with whom they have much more in common.

Change along republican lines will only come if ordinary members of these organizations decide to act, and to bring the principle of equality into the structure of the organizations to which they belong. Only those at the bottom of a hierarchy stand to gain unambiguously from greater equality. Where a few administrators try to keep tens or hundreds of thousands of members quiet and forthcoming with their dues, spontaneous speech menaces the existing order, with its steep slopes of power and pleasure. There is fine food and wine in the great charities of England. But most who pay the bills neither eat nor drink. I vividly recall meeting a diplomat at a Penguin authors' party more than a decade ago. He told me he was nearing retirement and looking for his next job. 'I've go my eye on the RSPB', he said. When I asked, somewhat naively, whether he had always been interested in bird conservation, he replied simply, 'Excellent dining'. ˙

The genteel rackets of the charitable sector stand as particular insults to the principle of equality in speech, but the leaders of all organizations will always be tempted to side with the existing order if the alternative is some loss of their freedom. Managed decline is more pleasing to managers than an unmanageable vitality. If we wait for our leaders to take up the great cause we will wait forever. But you may be sure that they will move rapidly if they see events slipping from their grasp.

At present those who have power and want to keep it become the advocates and agents of inequality. Inequality secures for them the gratifying burdens of command. Inequality makes the unprepossessing charismatic. Our equals do not excite us to raptures, but the applause of a people kept in ignorance is still applause. Leaders of opinion and of organizations must work with others similarly blessed and make common cause. They may disagree sharply in their publicised encounters but they have the same, unstated, practical concern: to remain consequential, to have the world confirm them in their worth. And in this way nominally representative and accountable institutions become as effectively hostile to popular freedom as the monarchies and aristocracies they replaced.

When politicians speak to us they offer the same wheedling reassurances as a Victorian poisoner. They would love us to run free, to play outside. But we are frail and pettish and plagued with absurd suspicions. We must stay where we can be properly looked after. Then they feed us whatever they can find to keep us shaky and confused. We learn that we are incapable of freedom, that our fellow citizens are feckless chavs, racist bigots or unforgiveable snobs. We need to be protected from ourselves and from each other.

Our incompetence is precious to our rulers, since it makes them indispensable. It doesn't matter that they deprive us of the information we need if we are to become competent, since we are not able to make use of it. They have to believe that we are incapable of government. What are they for, otherwise? The professional right feeds the bigotry of the excluded majority and the professional left regrets that the bigotry of the excluded means they must remain outside. The only sure safeguard against prejudice is knowledge of each other that our leaders cannot permit us to have. Similarly, the only basis for shared prosperity is knowledge of the world that would disrupt their prerogative to decide.

Leaders of all kinds have come to luxuriate in the idea that they and they alone can discern the public interest. They labour, tirelessly and thanklessly, for their constituents and members, secure in the knowledge that they serve a higher calling. How wonderful it is, to do as one likes, in such gracious humility. They are on the other side of the mystery of freedom, looking out. In this they have each inherited a fragment of the shattered power of kings.

The great majority stands to gain from a change in conditions. But change will only come if we learn to act with others. To this end, we would be wise to familiarize ourselves with the principles and procedures that can be used to structure equality in speech. It is these that enable each person to speak with some expectation of being heard. But as more of us become familiar with the methods, and as assembly begins to take place in different social contexts, we will have to adapt them. The work is not easy and we are bound to make mistakes. But freedom will elude us if we do not act as though others are about as competent and well-intentioned as we are, and if we don't learn to appreciate the efforts other make for the common good.

Assembly in the broadest sense is a medium for communication that, in concert with interactive technologies, can build new coalitions of informed and motivated citizens. These coalitions will lie outside the control of the politicians and their backers. They will also escape the terms of reference preferred by the mass media. In sufficient numbers they will mark the beginning of the end for a social order that cannot justify itself in uninhibited inquiry. Assembly can be the means by which we revise our shared account of world and its possibilities. And by changing the distribution of knowledge, it can also be the means by which we make permanent changes in the distribution of power.[6]

The pursuit of consensus on the basis of a shared understanding helps us to discover our shared interests and to decide for ourselves what divides and unites us. When we act as equals we are no longer dependent on a media-political order that is committed to inequality. It is this commitment to inequality that makes the current organization so radically unreliable, since it permits a tiny minority to determine the limits of public discussion and, if need be, to insist on absurdities.

Our focus is on the existing sites of decision. We want to turn the shared attention of the assembled public to the operations of our media-political institutions. We want to shift civil society away from the swindle of representation towards participation in candour. All this is necessary, whether we want to frighten our leaders into doing what is needed to restore prosperity and make the public world a little safer for honest descriptions, or whether we want to make a much more thorough change to our shared life.

Either way, our needs and theirs do not coincide. If we are to become free then they will have to more closely supervised. If we are no longer to be degraded, they must no longer be so exalted. They are anxious to frustrate us if they can, of course. While if we force them to act, they will hasten to assure us that they were always intending to do what we want. Each concession to the demands of a free public will be presented as the final achievement of their own, splendidly disinterested, reason.

Much the same can be said of the media. The major broadcasters and most newspapers repeatedly fail to describe the world when the powerful prefer that they stay quiet. They did not notice that the state was lying to secure popular consent for its invasion of Iraq. They did not notice that the banking system was staggering drunkenly towards collapse. They did not notice that national newspapers were adopting the methods and morals of organized crime.

The structure of the system of communications is a matter of profound constitutional significance. A conversation about politics that is not also a conversation about communications is a very incomplete affair. Citizens need new powers of decision. These needs can be discovered in assembly but they will only be satisfied by changes that are inscribed in a new republican constitution.

Sustained speech between equals requires changes in the way information is gathered and shared. At a minimum our freedom requires that we exercise direct control over the subsidies that support journalism. The darkness that surrounds editorial decision-making must be illuminated if we are to understand the circumstances in which we try to make our lives.

The details of what we want are to be discovered through assemblies and associated gatherings. They will be subject to refinement and revision in the light of new information. And besides, the governing order must be thoroughly understood before it can be reformed. We are very far from knowing what we are dealing with. In the end the assemblies will decide what they decide. But if we want to live in a democracy, we will want to change the systems of communication, credit and corporate organization. The vast social and economic power conceded to a few by government cannot remain beyond the reach of assemblies set on establishing a democratic constitution.

Those who currently hoard power stand to lose unambiguously from a greater equality of freedom. The most powerful stand to lose most. Much that divides us at present is accidental, illusory, and useful to those who rule. But irreconcilable differences between people will never vanish. Revolutionaries will have to persuade a majority that what they propose is practical and desirable. I hope that they can see that their cause is best served by reforms to the systems of information. Until the information that most people rely on is clarified through the exertions of a free people, radicals will struggle to make themselves comprehensible, let alone persuasive. The form of the assembly can teach us a great deal and its limits have yet to be established. But it is the beginning, not the end, of a reformed politics.

Some prefer to reject the political and economic order as it exists, and to build a parallel society right now, based on equality and radical freedom. This is welcome, but it is not the only path that leads from the occupations and assemblies. Unless participation takes on representation directly, the political classes will remain free to do as they please, while crying crocodile tears over their failure to engage the young.

Radical equality can do far more than discover and enact a

series of political programmes. But the very considerable powers of persuasion in the hands of the politicians and the media will be used to estrange people from experiments in new forms of life. The majority cannot be so easily ushered away from a politics that delivers material improvements; more spacious and more plentiful housing, better transport, schools that prepare their pupils for life as free citizens. The republican focus on the sovereign central state is important here.

The state and its auxiliaries in the media spend vast sums keeping such possibilities away from general awareness. Consider for a moment what will survive the scrutiny of an undaunted people, and what will be found wanting. The polite fictions and evasions that pass for our shared knowledge will give way to a more unruly body of descriptions. Much that is now considered marginal or disreputable will become quite lustrously obtrusive. We will have to make a reckoning with what we discover, for all that we find it disconcerting. Once we know the world we can make sensible plans to change it. Until then we are the dupes of those who shape the content of our beliefs, who introduce us to each other as enemies and competitors, and who stand exalted on the shambles they create.

Conclusion

A Republican Style of Life

It appears to general observation, that revolutions create genius and talents; but those events do no more than bring them forward. There is existing in man, a mass of sense lying in a dormant state, and which, unless something excites it to action, will descend with him, in that condition, to the grave. As it is to the advantage of society that the whole of its faculties should be employed, the construction of government ought to be such as to bring forward, by a quiet and regular operation, all that extent of capacity which never fails to appear in revolutions.

Tom Paine

The British often use the word republic in ways that obscure what is interesting and useful about republican ideas. Many self-described republicans are committed to a programme that is not, as a matter of fact, republican. Meanwhile we are not even a formally sovereign people and this astonishing fact goes largely unremarked. The absence of a written constitution is only part of the country's strangeness. As R.H. Tawney put it, the country 'carried into the democratic era, not only the institutions, but the social habits and mentality of the oldest and toughest plutocracy in the world'. After hundreds of years of imperialism at home and in the wider world we are left with a highly centralised and financialised political economy. Without the encumbrance of a written and codified constitution the offshore empire flourishes. The rest of us no longer understand freedom as a collective achievement and look for consolation in loyalty to the established order. The Tesco clubcard miniaturises our subjection. We spend pounds and are grateful for pennies in return.

So Britain might seem like an unpromising place to attempt a republican transformation of the constitutional order. But this is where we live and, as the Swedes say, *gräv där du står* – dig where you stand. Most countries are republics in which a minority nevertheless rule. If a maximally republican political order can be established here, it can be established anywhere.

A republican movement for reform will have few friends in the established institutions. The parties that aspire to govern cannot stand outside the system to which they belong. Their overriding concern is effective competition within the Parliamentary nation. They are nervous of stepping outside the consensus established among the effectual public – a group that is wealthy, enjoys high status and refuses to believe that its wealth and status are legitimate objects for review, regardless that both are almost uniformly ill-gotten. Furthermore, republicanism at full stretch makes politicians uneasy. Remember Richard Crossman's point, that for most members of Wilson's Cabinet in the 1960s, 'the notion of creating the extra burden of a live and articulate public opinion able to criticise actively and make its own choices is something that most socialist politicians keenly resent'.[7] The inherited institutions and assumptions of a monarchical and aristocratic state are even more beguiling to modern politicians than they were to avowed socialists in the 1960s. People will not be given a chance to decide for themselves. They will have to take it.

The broadcasters and the rest of the major media stand to lose a great deal in a communications system based on public oversight and control. Other powerful institutions also want to protect themselves from the disruption they see in popular participation. The financial sector and its partners in the Treasury and the Bank of England will try to keep their arrangements incomprehensible to the great majority. Having crashed the car they are hoping that the passengers are too concussed to demand a look at the map, let alone a turn behind the wheel. Although the natural and human sciences are humiliated by their subordination to the needs of industry and a secretive state, many scientists, experts and academics still cling to their abusers. Like so many others in the offshore empire they accept slavery as the price of the despotic power they wield. The only basis for republicanism in Britain is the general population. If its advocates are sincere, they will take pains to distinguish themselves from anti-monarchists. Otherwise they put themselves in the shameful position of having to postpone progress towards greater democracy until the next messy royal divorce.

Besides, reformers should be wary of fighting the guardians of the established order on the terrain of sentiment. The lead singer of Talking Heads, David Byrne, could see that the patriotism of America under Reagan was 'a trick' but he did his best to fall for it. The radicalism of the sixties and seventies had defined itself against what the mainstream liked and found reassuring. 'We have been taught not to like things', Byrne said. 'Finally somebody said it was OK to like things. This was a great relief'.[8] Most of us aren't obviously more resistant to the appeal of tradition than the writer of 'Life During Wartime'. It is OK to like the monarchy.

A population starts to become a public when it organizes itself into bodies where individuals deliberate as equals about matters of shared concern. It takes another step when these bodies engage with each other on the basis of mutual recognition. Public communication of this kind leads to action in pursuit of shared objectives. This leads to further communication and further action. Over time the publics become sufficiently confident to address the existing institutions on terms that do not accept their definitions and prior assumptions. A republican movement aims to re-create the offices and powers of the state along lines that are acceptable to the majority of the population. It is a revolutionary project.

This is to put things in the abstract. Let's be a little more direct.

We will achieve public status when we discover what our fellow citizens think about the current situation, and when we work out with them how we want to change it. It isn't enough to set out elaborate abstract plans for republican reform. Such plans are yet more sales pitches in a culture that does not lack for them.

It will be much more interesting and rewarding to join with others in order to learn more about them and ourselves. As we learn more we can engage with the existing powers with greater confidence. We can occupy institutional spaces and re-organize them on the basis of republican common ownership. We can examine the regional and national media in the light of our own experience and decide how we want them to change. We can, politely but steadily, insist that broadcasters respond to our concerns about systemic bias and deference to the established order. We can engage with the electoral process in ways that do not succumb to Burke's pleasing illusions.

Every time we act reasonably and are dismissed unreasonably we will grow more plausible in the eyes of those who matter, our fellow citizens. Manipulative administration is no match for republican principle.

In Scotland citizens can use the referendum campaign to develop a republican programme that reaches beyond formal independence from the United Kingdom to full independence from the tyranny of finance and the political cartels. The rest of us, the English in particular, have some catching up to do. And England is the hard problem. It is, after all, both the last province of a residual empire and the capital of a new imperial project. This offshore empire flourishes in the gaps in general under-standing and serves the overlapping needs of otherwise antago-nistic elite projects elsewhere. It cannot survive if democratic republicanism is established in England.

Given the difficulty of challenging these arrangements it is tempting to distract ourselves with one form of pseudo-politics or another. We could have endless fun mocking the blind spots and prejudices of those who read different newspapers and make sense of the world in different ways. They can idle away their time doing much the same. But we could also set about creating a public culture that is open to all and that gains influence to the extent that it treats important issues more fully and more responsibly than the existing media. Such a culture will gain ground if it is founded on the recognition that people are reasonably well intentioned and at least intermittently willing to review their beliefs in the light of the best available evidence. As such it will concern itself more with the deceits of the powerful than with the deficiencies of the rest of us.

This isn't only a matter of putting pressure on institutions we do not control. While we cannot do very much on our own, together we can create the institutions we need. An individual is one more shopper in the supermarket aisle. An assembly is an embryonic buyers' cooperative, a collection of sellers' cooperatives, a credit union. An individual can decide not to give their money to companies that pay little or no tax. An assembly can underwrite co-operatives that pay their taxes and provide a surplus to fund projects that the public support. It can fund its own media outlets and use them to promote public liberty as a cause and as a form of life. Through assembly we can secure immediate changes to the structure of power, and so gain the energy and confidence to secure more.

Once the public discovers itself in shared endeavour it can address the institutions of unreformed private and state power. Like the supermarkets, the politicians currently engage with us as isolated individuals. They tell us to vote for them on their terms, take it or leave it. A republican public that dispenses with the pleasures of party affiliation and exchanges the charisma of the leader for the charisma of a programme can begin to set out the terms on which it will support the ambitions of individuals. In 2015 we could see republican movements – organized and articulate publics – in every constituency that decide whether to support one of the major party candidates, to support an established alternative, or to field their own. Such movements could begin to push the current crisis towards a resolution that favours the majority.

If we are sincere in our desire for a new constitutional order, and the new society and economy it implies, then we must be clear-eyed about the circumstances in which we find ourselves. There is not much support for abolition of the monarchy. Better by far, then, to build maximally republican institutions and use them - to alter the terrain on which the next general election is fought, but also to create new knowledge, new states of mind, new power.

Our aim, after all, is not victory in that or any other electoral contest. Our aim is a form of government that gives each of us both motive and means to exert ourselves to the full extent of our powers. Efforts to achieve this will make us more like the citizens of a free republic. In Britain this means paying close attention to the structures of the national, local and regional media. It means taking the electoral system seriously. It means learning to act as plausible successors of the rulers we say we want to replace.

There are perhaps a million socialists, anarchists and communists in Britain. This million is all but entirely irrelevant and will remain so until it begins to organize with a view to challenging Parliament for control of public opinion. As long as we limit ourselves to complaints about global capitalism in the abstract we will leave its concrete manifestations in Britain untouched. Once we begin to build republican institutions, in which people accept sovereign responsibility for their own lives, discover their shared interests and pursue them, we become politically significant. Until then we are no kind of threat.

Republicanism offers us a language of individual virtue and a programme of structural change. By recasting the state as a property held in common it compels us to think in ways that reach beyond liberal constitutionalism. It offers those currently excluded – by geography, ethnicity, age or gender – a space to create an alternative that does not imply retreat from the political sphere. Most importantly, republican institutions offer the best venue for debate about change.

Those who complain that such a programme is insufficiently radical should think again. Republican democracy fully realised means the end of capitalism in fact, not theory. There's no need for blood-curdling rhetoric. Efforts to create a maximally republican constitution challenge the oligarchy directly. They will not say so. If the oligarchs deign to notice us at first they will claim to be indifferent or amused. Meanwhile they will noisily pretend to be frightened of the kind of revolution that will never happen, the prospect of which they keep alive with police subsidies. Let's pay the effectual public the compliment of ignoring what they say and copying what they do. They currently control the state and most consequential speech. It is up to us to put both in the hands of a sovereign people.

You don't really need me to tell you how late it is, or what will happen if we don't create a maximally republican form of government. You've read this far, after all. But you will not persuade the great majority that a maximum republic is possible, until you stop fooling yourself that anti-monarchism and republicanism are the same thing. You will not persuade your fellow citizens that a system of popular oversight and control will work until they see it working before their eyes. You will not persuade them of the merits of a republican style of life until they see the change that the pursuit of public liberty makes in you.

So it is time to stop fretting about kings and see the Magic Kingdom for what it is. If we are serious about wanting significant change of any kind, and we are serious about democracy, then we want a republic equal to our times. No one will make it for us. Plenty of people will tell us that we are not ready, that we never will be. We are not ready, but we will be. It is by freeing ourselves that we become equal to the demands of liberty

Acknowledgements and Further Reading

The Magic Kingdom is a revised and expanded version of *Maximum Republic*, an e-book published in the Autumn of 2012. Chapter 5 draws on the remarks on assembly in an e-book published earlier that year, *Common Sense: Occupation, Assembly and the Future of Liberty*.

I would like to thank Olly Huitson, Antony Barnett and Stuart White for their thoughtful comments on various versions of the text. An openDemocracy project on the 'digital commons' gave me a chance to think more carefully about modern forms of enclosure. Stuart White's article 'The Republican critique of capitalism' encouraged me to think about the ways in anarchism and socialism relate to the republican tradition. It deserves the widest possible readership among those interested in the forms a post-capitalist future might take.

Tony Wright's *Very Short Introduction to British Politics* and Martin Loughlin's *Very Short Introduction to the British Constitution* helped me immeasurably in my attempts to grapple the squid that is the contemporary British system. As in my previous work I have also leant heavily on Quentin Skinner's *Liberty Before Liberalism*.

My description of the contemporary offshore empire owes a great deal to Nicholas Shaxson's *Treasure Islands* and Richard Brook's *The Great Tax Robbery*. I have also benefited greatly from the tireless efforts of John Christensen and Richard Murphy to trace the outlines of the offshore world.

Tom Nairn's *The Enchanted Glass* and Anthony Barnett's *Iron Britannia* are indispensable reading for anyone attempting to understand the thought-world of the unreformed political system. Larry Siedentop's *Democracy in Europe* first brought me to appreciate the strangeness of the British arrangements.

Needless to say, while I have borrowed freely, any errors are my own.

Mark Fisher, Tariq Goddard, Liam Sprod and Alex Niven made the publishing process simple and enjoyable, in spite of my best efforts. I am very grateful, as ever, to my friends Rebecca Fox and Jake Osborne for their friendship and encouragement, and to my parents Diana and Geoffrey Hind for their support throughout my life, and especially in the last few months.

Finally I would like to thank the many people who have shown me over the years that, for all our faults, we are still our best hope.

London, January, 2014.

Notes

Prologue: A Constitutional Crisis

1. The BBC has removed the news item in question from its website. But it can be found on Youtube in the first episode of the first series of Charlie Brooker's Newswipe. The relevant section comes at 7 minutes and 9 seconds into this clip – http://www.youtube.com/watch?v=n886PlxwJS8&feature=player_detailpage#t=392s%29

2. See, for example, 'Anti-cuts march in Manchester: More than 35,000 attend', BBC News, October 2nd, 2011. Baroness Warsi is quoted saying that 'we're making sure that this generation does not bankrupt the next. Not saddling them with our debts, not maxing out on the nation's credit card, but building a better future for our children'.

3. A mis-selling scandal is a fraud. A mis-pricing scandal is a fraud.

Introduction: The Needs of Oligarchy

1. 'David Cameron's new year message', *Guardian*, 2 January, 2012,

2. Tom Clark, 'Queen enjoys record support in *Guardian*/ICM poll', *Guardian*, 24 May, 2012.

3. 'Support for monarchy is at all time high', Ipsos Mori, 28 May, 2012.

4. Patrick Wintour, 'Cameron announces £50m fund for First World War commemorations', *Guardian*, 11 October, 2012. Fittingly, we recently learnt that the Foreign Office files covering the period before the outbreak of the Great War are still classified. We are being asked to commemorate something we don't understand.

5. Of course some of the framers of the US constitution always intended that America's republican institutions would act as

hosts for a nascent empire. But the revolutionary movement against the Crown in America included radical democrats and anti-imperialists.

6. I asked the Palace whether the Queen would accept the position of head of state in a formal constitution in which power derives from the people. The Palace's spokesman, David Pogson, replied to say that 'as Head of State The Queen has to remain strictly neutral with respect to all political matters, and I would refer you to Parliament for any comments regarding the Constitution'.

7. In the Ipsos Mori poll noted above pollsters asked a thousand people 'would you favour Britain becoming a republic or remaining a monarchy?' The option of a substantially republican constitution with a crowned head of state was not offered. Its absence is the space in which this book is intended to fit.

8. As we shall see, this is a point well grasped by those, like David Hume and Edmund Burke, who wished to preserve the rule of property.

9. Internationalists who imagine that they have transcended nationalism are all too often playing out the grandest pretensions towards universal status of a national project. Disdain for the nation as an object of affection or opportunity for shared sentiment is, I think, one of the last, heavily mutated, forms of the British imperial mind.

10. Edmund Burke, *Burke's Thoughts on the Present Discontents* (London: Macmillan, 1902), p.8.

11. Christopher Hitchens, *The Monarchy: A Critique of Britain's Favourite Fetish* (London: Chatto and Windus, 1990, 2012).

12. That is actually true, by the way. You'd need about 168 billion loaves 33 centimetres long to build a tower of bread and butter 56 billion metres high to Mars. Another 168 billion loaves would build you a tower of bread back. Assuming each loaf costs a pound, you'd have £39 billion left to spend

on butter.

13. Geoffrey Ingham, *Capitalism Divided? The City and Industry in British Social Development* (Houndsmills: Macmillan, 1984), p.xx.

14. Walter Wriston is quoted in Anthony Sampson, *The Money Lenders* (London: Penguin, 1983), p.142.

15. Well, the specter of uselessness, to be exact, Sennett being an American. See Richard Sennett, *The Culture of the New Capitalism* (Yale University Press: New Haven, 2006).

16. A maximally republican system promises more than material improvement. It promises the end of the monopoly on glory held by a few. It makes glory a common possession. Besides, the only glory worth a damn derives from the reasoned approval of a free people.

Chapter 1: A Time-Honoured Improvisation

1. See Tony Wright, *British Politics: A Very Short Introduction* (Oxford: Oxford University Press, 2003), p.6.

2. Alexis de Tocqueville, *Democracy in America* (London: Fontana, 1994), p.101.

3. Thomas Paine, *Rights of Man and Common Sense* (London: Verso, 2009), p.98

4. Tom Bingham, *The Rule of Law* (London: Allen Lane, 2010), p.162.

5. *The Cabinet Manual: A Guide to Laws. Conventions and Rules on the Operation of Government*, October, 2011, p.2-3.

6. *The House of Lords – Completing the Reform, A Government White Paper*, November 7, 2011. See Tony Wright, op. cit., p.50-1 for a useful discussion.

7. Ferdinand Mount, *The New Few, or A Very British Oligarchy* (London, Simon and Schuster, 2012), p.10.

8. Andrew Rawnsley, *Servants of the People: The Inside Story of New Labour* (London: Hamish Hamilton, 2000), p.33.

9. See Vernon Bogdanor, *The New British Constitution* (Oxford:

Hart, 2009) for an argument along these lines.

10. See Bingham, op. cit., pp.160-70 for an accessible and author-itative treatment of this point.

11. Martin Loughlin, *The British Constitution: A Very Short Introduction* (Oxford: Oxford University Press, 2013), p.12. The Kirkwood quotation comes from David Kirkwood, *My Life of Revolt* (George G. Harrap: London, 1935), p.201-2. The Churchill quotation comes from the introduction to the same book, p.v.

12. Edmund Burke, *Works* (London: Samuel Holdsworth, 1837), p.124.

13. David Hume, *Selected Essays* (Oxford: Oxford University Press, 2008), p.24.

14. Edmund Burke, *Works* (London: Samuel Holdsworth, 1837), p.134.

15. Larry Siedentop, *Democracy in Europe* (London: Allen Lane, 2000), p.66.

16. See 'Theresa May: Health tourism "not fair"', *Today*, Radio 4, October 10th, 2013, for example. Online at: http://www.bbc.co.uk/news/uk-24471679 Her performance is discussed by Nick Cohen in 'In Theresa May's surreal world, feelings trump facts', *Observer*, October 12, 2013. Given the state of public opinion regarding, say, nationalisation, the preference for feelings over facts is perhaps understandable.

17. Edmund Burke, *Reflections on the Revolution in France* (London: Penguin, 1968), p.239.

18. Walter Bagehot, *The English Constitution* (Oxford: Oxford University Press, 2009), p.103.

19. Walter Bagehot, op. cit., p.41.

20. Walter Bagehot, op. cit., p.186.

21. Walter Bagehot, op. cit., p.54.

22. Walter Bagehot, op. cit., p.122.

23. Walter Bagehot, op. cit., p.35.

Chapter 2: CSI: UK

1. The phrase comes from a leaked memo by Tony Blair. See Dan Hind, *The Return of the Public* (London: Verso, 2010), p.103.

2. During the 2013 party conferences the Liberal Democrats, Labour and the Conservatives started setting out their stalls for the 2015 election.

3. Gregory Elliott, *Labourism and the English Genius: The Strange Death of Labour England?* (London: Verso, 1993), p.43.

4. See the discussion in chapter 1 about the absence of restrictions on constitutional change. The 1945 election victory was enough to secure extensive changes in Britain's political economy. The Labour party began to dismantle it in the late 70s without the formality of a vote. After her victory in 1979 Thatcher finished the job.

5. Richard Crossman, *The Diaries of a Cabinet Minister, Volume 2* (London: Hamish Hamilton and Jonathan Cape, 1976), p.50.

6. Anthony Sampson, *The Essential Anatomy of Britain: Democracy in Crisis* (Sevenoaks: Coronet, 1993), p.123.

7. When Labour handed responsibility for setting interests rates to a committee at the Bank of England in 1997 its behaviour was entirely in keeping the party's tradition of baffled deference to the financial orthodoxy.

8. Quoted in Robin Ramsay, 'The Two Goulds', *Lobster*, 63. Anyone who is interested in escaping from the official version of British history would be well advised to read Ramsay's essays in *Lobster*, or his long essay *Well, How Did We Get Here? A Brief History of the British Economy, Minus the Wishful Thinking* (London: Commonwealth Publishing, 2012).

9. Aeron Davis, 'News of the Financial Sector: reporting on the City or to it?', openDemocracy, May 31st, 2011.

10. See, for example, Mike Berry, 'The Today programme and the banking crisis', *Journalism*, September 27th, 2012.

11. That said, many MPs are buy-to-let landlords, a sector that has become a kind of nursery for exploitation.

12. Tom Paine, ibid.

13. Kearney was talking on 'World at One', Radio 4, July 9th, 2013, online at http://audioboo.fm/boos/1493048-people-estimate-that-34-times-more-benefit-money-is-claimed-fraudulently-than-official-estimates

14. Gerald Kaufman was speaking at 'OurBeeb Forum session 2: Accountability and the Savile Scandal', December 4th, 2012. The video can be seen online at http://www.open democracy.net/ourbeeb/dan-hind-anthony-barnett-gerald-kaufman/ourbeeb-forum-session-2-accountability-and-savile-sc

15. Tony Dolphin, *Don't Bank On It: The Financialisation of the UK Economy*, IPPR, December, 2012, p.18.

16. For figures on bank lending, see Ann Pettifor, *Sound Money* (Commonwealth: London, 2014). For private sector debt, see 'Red Ink Rising: How Worrying is the UK Economy's Total Debt Burden?', UK Economic Outlook, November 2010. Online at http://www.pwcwebcast.co.uk/ukeo_nov2010_debt.pdf

17. John Thanassoulis, 'Supermarket Profitability Investigation', University of Oxford, January 2009, p.3.

18. Rebecca Roberts-Hughes, *The Case for Space*, Royal Institute of British Architects, September 2011, p.11. The figures for 'guard labour' come from Will Hutton, 'So Europe is a write-off?' Beware those economic forecasts ...', *Observer*, December 29, 2013.

19. 'Economists define rents as excess returns that accrue as a result of positional advantage in a market, for example as a result of exploiting a monopoly, or patent rights, or information not available to other participants in the market' Tony Dolphin, *Don't Bank On It: The Financialisation of the UK Economy*, IPPR, December, 2012, p.3.

The Democratic Audit data can be found on the *Guardian* website at http://www.theguardian.com/news/datablog/20 12/jul/06/politics-democracy-decline-audit-data

For the 'get-rich-quick scheme' comment, see 'BBC Savile scoop journalist Liz MacKean says corporation has become "get rich quick scheme" for "officer class"', *Press Gazette*, 23 August, 2013.

20. John Kay was speaking on 'How You Pay for the City', episode 1, first broadcast August 3, 2013.

21. Stuart Weir, 'UK becomes the world second largest outsourcing market', openDemocracy, March 29, 2013. http://www.opendemocracy.net/ourkingdom/stuart-weir/uk-becomes-worlds-second-largest-outsourcing-market

22. Quoted in Richard Cockett, *Thinking the Unthinkable* (London: Fontana, 1995), p.272-5. Jim Callaghan told an adviser in 1979 that 'there are times, perhaps once every 30 years, when there is a sea change in politics ... I suspect there is now such a sea change – and it is for Mrs Thatcher'. It would be interesting to know if Callaghan had seen a copy of *Stepping Stones*, the 1977 memo where Hoskyns uses the phrase.

23. Özlem Onaran and Giorgos Galanis, 'Is aggregate demand wage-led or profit-led? National and global effects', Conditions of Work and Employment Series, No. 40, International Labour Office, p.4-5

24. Ed Balls, 'Speech by the Economic Secretary to the Treasury to the Hong Kong General Chambers of Commerce and the British Chamber of Commerce', September 13th, 2006.

25. Jeremy Hetherington-Gore, 'UK PLC Heads for the Exit', *Tax-News*, 20th October, 2006. Needless to say, the financiers responded to Brown's warm words by threatening to relocate offshore.

26. Of course, many of them have been educated in the same, or

similar, schools and universities.

27. The Minister for Aviation and Shipping, quoted in Warwick Funnell, Robert Jupe and Jane Andrew, *In Government We Trust: Market Failure and the Delusions of Privatization* (London: Pluto, 2009), p.16.

28. 'State-run railway beats private rivals', Mark Odell, *Financial Times*, April 18, 2013.

29. Massimo Florio, *The Great Divestiture* (London: MIT Press, 2004), pp. 341-2.

30. See Geoffrey Ingham, *Capitalism Divided? The City and Industry in British Social Development* (Houndsmills: Macmillan, 1984) for an account of the City's historical role in the global economy.

31. House of Commons Political and Constitutional Reform Committee, 'Do We Need A Constitutional Convention for the UK?', HC 371, March p.18.

32. Anna Minton, 'Scaring the Living Daylights Out of People: The Local Lobby and the Failure of Democracy', Spinwatch, March 2013, p.19.

33. Quoted by Greg Philo in 'Television, Politics, and the New Right', available online at www.gla.ac.uk. Mandelson's remarks come from his evidence to the House of Common Select Committee on the European Union's Inquiry on Transatlantic Trade and Investment Partnership, October 31st, 2013.

34. Sharon Beder, *Power Play: The Fight for Control of the World's Electricity* (Victoria: Scribe, 2003), p. 221.

35. 'Report by The Rt. Hon. The Lord Mayor (Mr Alderman John Stuttard) on his visit to India, Saturday 19 May-Saturday 26 May 2007', quoted in Ingrid Hauge Johansen, 'The Role of the City of London Corporation and Lord Mayor in the Global Financial Crisis', visar.csustan.edu/aaba/Johansen 2012.pdf

36. ibid.

37. See Ed Howker and Shiv Malik, 'David Cameron's family fortune: the Jersey, Panama and Geneva Connection', *Guardian*, April 20th, 2012.

38. 'NM Rothschild pitches motorway privatization plan', Robert Watts and Dominic O'Connell, *Sunday Times*, August 30th, 2009. At the time the Liberal politician Vince Cable called the Rothschild proposals 'an attractive, positive idea which could release considerable resources to the public finances and may have real environmental merits. The scale of it is vast – it makes rail privatisation look like small beer'.

39. Bernard Porter, 'Other People's Mail', *London Review of Books*, November 19th, 2009.

40. For Le Carré's comments, see 'Conversations with John le Carré', Philippe Sands, *Financial Times*, September 6th, 2013. For McBride's account, see 'Damian McBride was asked about "deviant sexual practices" by kindly aunt', *Guardian*, September 27th, 2013.

41. 'Memorandum Submitted by the City of London Corporation', Office of the City Remembrancer, May 2007.

42. 'Speech by the Chancellor of the Exchequer, Rt Hon George Osborne, MP, at the City of London RMB launch event', April 18, 2012. Online at http://www.hm-treasury.gov.uk/speech_chx_180412.htm

The Chinese government is probably less keen on the idea.

43. Aristotle, *Nicomachean Ethics* (Oxford: Oxford University Press, 2009), p.4.

44. Allen is quoted in 'Britain to take a major step towards written constitution', Christopher Hope, *Telegraph*, December 13th, 2011.

45. Anthony Barnett, 'An Empire State' in Anthony Barnett (ed.) *Power and the Throne* (Vintage, 1994), p.34.

46. Earl John Russell, *An Essay on the History of the English Government and Constitution* (Longman et al , 1823) p.255. A

reformed constitution will have important implications for the country's system of education.

47. For a while it looked like that would be the end of the matter but a series of civil cases and some sure-footed reporting by the *Guardian* led to an outcry, a judge-led inquiry and some proposals for press reform.

48. Niccolò Machiavelli, *Discourses on Livy* (Oxford: Oxford University Press, 2008), pp.79-80.

49. Of course, *pace* Pogson, the current dynasty might refuse to become a normal monarchy, in which case the people can do what the oligarchs did when it suited them and find a replacement.

50. Anthony Barnett (ed.), *Power and the Throne* (London: Vintage, 1994), p.147. Wainwright argues that abolition of the monarchy is a necessary but not sufficient condition for a republic. I would say that it is unnecessary. Its retention, on the other hand, might be a practical necessity.

51. Anthony Barnett op cit., p.70

52. Quoted in Quentin Skinner, 'Rethinking Political Liberty', *History Workshop Journal*, 61, Spring, 2006, pp.156-70. Henry Parker was himself a Member of Parliament.

Chapter 3: Republican Principles

1. Abraham Lincoln, 'Speech on the Kansas-Nebraska Act', March 21st, 1854, available online at http://www.vlib.us/amdocs/texts/kansas.html

2. Eleanor Roosevelt and Allida M. Black, *Courage in a Dangerous World: The Political Writings of Eleanor Roosevelt* (New York: Columbia, 2000), p.244.

3. Colin Leys, *Total Politics: Market Politics, Market State* (Monmouth: Merlin Press, 2008), p.99.

4. I am grateful to Jamie Stern-Weiner for pointing out the distinction.

5. Niccolò Machiavelli, *The Discourses on Livy* (Oxford: Oxford

University Press, 2008), p.33.

6. Ronald Syme, *The Roman Revolution* (Oxford: Oxford University Press, 1960), p.53. Syme was describing Caesar's freedom outside Rome.

7. Of course, misogyny and contempt for the mild have not left the ruling class. They are no longer expressed quite so frankly, that's all.

8. See Walter Karp, *The Politics of War The Story of Two Wars Which Altered Forever the Political Life of the American Republic* (New York: Franklin Square Press, 2003)

9. I don't presume to know exactly *how* the public will define and constrain state power. In what follows I only try to explain what arrangements are necessary if it is to be capable of doing so.

10. Undated interview of Dick Costolo by Martin Nisenholtz at Riptide – http://www.niemanlab.org/riptide/person/dick-costolo/

11. See Bruce A. Williams and Michael X. Carpini, *After Broadcast News: Media Regimes, Democracy and the New Informaiton Environment* (Cambridge: Cambridge University Press, 2011) and Robert McChesney, *Digital Disconnect: How Capitalism is Turning the Internet Against Democracy* (New York: The New Press, 2013).

12. Walter Lippmann, *Public Opinion* (New York: Simon and Schuster, 1997), p.171.

13. But this is starting to change, see the note above on media regimes.

14. Aristotle, *Nichomachean Ethics* (Oxford: Oxford University Press, 2009), p.4.

15. James Harrington, *The Commonwealth of Oceana* (London: Routledge, 1887), p.18.

16. James Harrington, op. cit., p.39-40.

17. John Curl, *For All the People: Uncovering the Hidden History of Cooperation, Cooperative Movements and Communalism in*

America (Oakland: PM Press, 2012), p.354. Webster's thought remains heavily influenced by classical ideas about the connections between property and civic virtue. In his eyes the 'laborious and saving' should retain both property and power since they are 'generally the best citizens'. Eighteenth-century republicans were not, for the most part, egalitarian democrats. And rather than tackle the concentration of property, the framers of the American constitution preferred to break up popular sovereignty through a multiplicity of antagonistic jurisdictions, the better to protect the propertied from everyone else.

18. The Omaha Platform was established as the party programme of the Populists on July 4th, 1892. The text can be read online at http://historymatters.gmu.edu/d/5361/

19. Irving Dilliard, *Mr Justice Brandeis: Great American* (St Louis: Modern View Press, 1941), p.42.

20. 'Clinton Urges Action on Bills to Create Jobs, Lift Incomes', *New York Times*, March 5, 1996.

21. Thelwall is quoted in Stuart White, 'The Republican critique of capitalism', *Critical Review of International Social and Political Philosophy*, 14:5 (2011), p.567.

Chapter 4: Maximum Republic

1. See Dan Hind *The Return of the Public* (London: Verso, 2010) for a fuller account of public commissioning.

2. Again, see Bruce A. Williams and Michael X. Delli Carpini, *After Broadcast News: Media Regimes, Democracy and the New Information Environment* (New York: Cambridge University Press, 2011) for a recent discussion of this in the US context.

3. 'In Defence of Politics', Radio 4, Episode 2, 3 October, 2011. Blair thinks that the media are too cynical about politicians and politics, and that there is too great an emphasis on personalities instead of policies. But the journalists take their cues from the politicians and the current coverage of politics

reflects the wishes of the leading figures in Parliament. http://www.bbc.co.uk/programmes/b015bxqs

4. Harvey Brooks, *The Government of Science* (Cambridge: MIT Press, 1968), p.28.

5. Donald Fisher, *Fundamental Development of the Social Sciences: Rockefeller Philanthropy and the United States Research Council* (Ann Arbor: University of Michigan Press, 1993), p.71.

6. See Peter Hennessy, *The Secret State* (London: Allen Lane, 2002), p.208-9 for a particularly hair-rising example of this habit of mind.

7. Paul Samuelson, quoted by L. Randall Wray in 'Modern Money: The Way that a Sovereign Currency "Works"'. The presentation is online at: http://www.youtube.com/watch?v=0zEbo8PIPSc

8. Quoted in Michael R. King 'Distributional Politics and Central Bank Independence: New Labour's Reform of the Bank of England' March 2003 draft, p.15.

9. Geoffrey Robinson, *An Unconventional Minister* (London: Michael Joseph, 2000), p.36.

10. 'Bank of England "Deliberately Fostered Personal Debt" to Avert Recession', *Daily Mail*, March 20, 2007.

11. I am writing this in November 2013.

12. Those who wonder why the world is largely owned and run by clever, self-assured, and supremely self-centred, middle aged men might want to start their inquiries here.

13. Martin Wolf, *Why Globalization Works* (London: Yale University Press, 2005), p.298.

14. See Stuart White, 'The Republican critique of capitalism', *Critical Review of International Social and Political Philosophy* (2011), 14:5, 561-579

15. Oddsdóttir's is quoted in Dan Hind, 'A constitution for Europe', June 6, 2012. http://www.aljazeera.com/indepth/opinion/2012/06/2012658135998757.html

Chapter 5: From Here to There

1. Tom Paine, *The Rights of Man and Common Sense* (London: Verso, 2009), p.87.

2. 'The Snowden Files', John Lanchester, *Guardian*, October 3rd, 2013.

3. Edmund Burke, *Thoughts on the Causes of the Present Discontents* (Macmillan: London, 1902), p.51.

4. In my experience, speaking in an assembly is somewhat more difficult than speaking on a platform as an invited speaker. But it is much easier – and more pleasant – to speak in an assembly than to speak from the floor in a conventionally structured meeting.

5. Do we want to act as atomised voters, or as members of self-conscious and reasoning publics? That's the question each of us must answer.

6. It is tempting to overstate the degree to which the population is uninformed about the world. But it is fair to say that we are very poorly informed about each other.

7. Richard Crossman, *The Diaries of a Cabinet Minister, Volume 2* (London: Hamish Hamilton and Jonathan Cape, 1976), p.50.

8. James Verini, 'The Talking Heads Song that Explains Talking Heads', *New Yorker* online, June 14, 2012.

Contemporary culture has eliminated both the concept of the public and the figure of the intellectual. Former public spaces – both physical and cultural – are now either derelict or colonized by advertising. A cretinous anti-intellectualism presides, cheerled by expensively educated hacks in the pay of multinational corporations who reassure their bored readers that there is no need to rouse themselves from their interpassive stupor. The informal censorship internalized and propagated by the cultural workers of late capitalism generates a banal conformity that the propaganda chiefs of Stalinism could only ever have dreamt of imposing. Zer0 Books knows that another kind of discourse – intellectual without being academic, popular without being populist – is not only possible: it is already flourishing, in the regions beyond the striplit malls of so-called mass media and the neurotically bureaucratic halls of the academy. Zer0 is committed to the idea of publishing as a making public of the intellectual. It is convinced that in the unthinking, blandly consensual culture in which we live, critical and engaged theoretical reflection is more important than ever before.